AMERICA'S TOP 100

Edward Ricciuti

Jenny Tesar

Tanya Lee Stone

BLACKBIRCH PRESS, INC.

WOODBRIDGE, CONNECTICUT

Published by Blackbirch Press, Inc.
260 Amity Road
Woodbridge, CT 06525

©2000 by Blackbirch Press, Inc.
First Edition

e-mail: staff@blackbirch.com
Web site: www.blackbirch.com

Printed in the United States of America.

10 9 8 7 6 5 4 3 2 1

Library of Congress Cataloging-in-Publication Data
Ricciuti, Edward R.
[1st ed.]
America's Top 100 / by Edward Ricciuti, Jenny Tesar, Tanya Lee Stone.
        p.   cm.
        Includes bibliographical references (p. 228) and index.
        ISBN 1-56711-151-3
        1. Historic sites—United States—Juvenile literature. 2. United States—History, Local Miscellanea—Juvenile literature. 3. Curiosities and Wonders—United States—Juvenile literature. I. Tesar, Jenny E. II. Title. III. Title: America's top one-hundred
E159.R53   2000   99-35827
973—dc21   CIP
                                                                                                AC

TABLE OF CONTENTS

AMERICA'S TOP
10
BRIDGES

Manhattan

East River

**Brooklyn
Bridge**

Brooklyn

The
Brooklyn Bridge

No American bridge has been more celebrated in songs, stories, and poetry than the Brooklyn Bridge. This grand structure spans New York City's East River and connects the boroughs of Brooklyn and Manhattan. The bridge is known for the majesty of its stone approaches and granite towers. Between its towers, the Brooklyn Bridge has a main span of 1,595 feet, which made it the world's longest suspension bridge when it was completed in 1883. Suspension bridges have roadways that hang by steel "suspenders" from steel cables. These, in turn, are held up by a pair of towers.

When the bridge was built, Brooklyn and New York were separate cities. Both were thriving business centers. The only way to cross the East River that flowed between them was by ferry. During the very cold winter of 1866–67, ice made it difficult to run the ferry service, and the decision was made to build a bridge over the East River.

J.A. Roebling and his son designed the Brooklyn Bridge using technology that was brand new at the time. It was the first suspension bridge to hang from cables of steel wire. With an average clearance of 133 feet above high tide, the bridge was high enough to allow ocean-going vessels— both sailboats and steam-powered ones—to pass underneath.

Almost as soon as the bridge was opened, it became a popular spot for weekend strollers. In 1964, the bridge was designated a National Historic Landmark.

Location: Between Brooklyn and Manhattan in New York City
Type: Suspension
Body of water spanned: East River
Opened: May 24, 1883
Length: Suspended structure 3,400 feet; main span 1,595 feet
Construction time: 13 years
Cost: $9 million
Fun fact: The main cables of the bridge are 16 inches thick.

Opposite page:
The Brooklyn Bridge is known for the beauty of its granite towers.

AMERICA'S TOP

10

BRIDGES

Chesapeake Bay

13

Chesapeake Bay Bridge-Tunnel

Virginia Beach

Atlantic Ocean

The Chesapeake Bay Bridge-Tunnel

★ ★ ★ ★ ★ ★ ★   ★ ★ ★ ★ ★ ★ ★

The Chesapeake Bay Bridge-Tunnel (also known as the Lucius J. Kellam, Jr., Bridge-Tunnel) is considered one of the greatest engineering projects in the world. It is also the world's largest bridge-tunnel. It connects the Eastern Shore of Virginia with the rest of the state. The Eastern Shore is located at the southern end of a peninsula—land that juts out into the water. This part of Virginia is cut off from the rest of the state by Maryland and Delaware, to the north, and by the mouth of Chesapeake Bay, to the south. When the Chesapeake Bay Bridge-Tunnel opened in 1964, motorists could drive from the Eastern Shore to mainland Virginia in only 25 minutes.

This great engineering achievement is a combination of trestles, 2 tunnels, and 2 high-level bridges. Together they stretch 17.6 miles across the entrance to Chesapeake Bay. The waterways over the tunnels form an important route for naval vessels heading for bases on the Virginia mainland. Tunnels were built because in time of war, bridges in that area might be destroyed, blocking the channel.

The 2 high-level bridges are over smaller shipping channels. The North Channel Bridge, the largest, provides a clearance of 75 feet for passing ships. The other, the Fisherman Inlet Bridge, has a 40-foot clearance.

Construction of the bridge-tunnel began in the fall of 1960 and took over 4 years. In 1987, the bridge-tunnel was officially named for Lucius J. Kellam, Jr., who led the effort to build it.

Location: Between Hampton Roads, Virginia, and Virginia's Eastern Shore

Type: Complex of concrete trestles, 2 tunnels, and 2 high-level bridges

Bodies of water spanned: Chesapeake Bay and Atlantic Ocean

Opened: April 15, 1964

Length: Shore-to-shore: 17.6 miles

Construction time: 42 months

Cost: $200 million

Fun fact: Since it opened, more than 60 million vehicles have crossed the bridge-tunnel.

Opposite page:
The Chesapeake Bay Bridge-Tunnel is the largest bridge-tunnel in the world.

AMERICA'S TOP

10

BRIDGES

Pacific
Ocean

101

North
Bend

Coos Bay Bridge

Coos Bay

The Coos Bay Bridge

★ ★ ★ ★ ★ ★ ★ ★ ★ ★ ★ ★ ★ ★ ★

This spectacular bridge (also known as the McCullough Bridge) across Oregon's Coos Bay was designed as a major link in coastal Highway 101 along the Oregon coast. Construction of the bridge began in 1934, on July 25. It was the last of 5 bridges built for Highway 101 between 1934 and 1936. When it was opened, the Coos Bay Bridge was the longest in the state. Today, the bridge is still a vital link in the Oregon highway system. An average of 15,900 vehicles per day cross the single deck of this bridge.

The structure is named after its designer, Conde B. McCullough, a well-known highway engineer. He played a key role in creating the state's modern highway system. The bridge across Coos Bay opened in 1936. To make the bridge, workers used 51,000 cubic yards of concrete, 2,205 tons of reinforced steel, and 3,635 tons of structural steel. In 1947, a year after McCullough died, the bridge was dedicated to his memory. It is one of the few bridges in the world to be named after its designer.

The Coos Bay Bridge is known for its clean design, which is very pleasing to the eye. The bridge has 3 spans. The center—the major portion of the bridge—is a 1,709-foot cantilever structure. Its center span is 793 feet long between the piers. This part of the bridge has a clearance of 180 feet above the water, to allow large ships to pass beneath it. This main bridge is connected to shore by 13 spans supported by reinforced-concrete arches.

Location: North Bend, Oregon
Type: Cantilever; concrete arch
Body of water spanned: Coos Bay
Opened: August 9, 1936
Length: Cantilever with span 1,709 feet; total 5,305 feet
Construction time: 2 years
Cost: $2.9 million
Fun fact: Building the bridge required a total of 789,040 hours of human labor.

Opposite page:
The center span of the Coos Bay Bridge is a cantilever structure.

AMERICA'S TOP

10

BRIDGES

Seattle

Lake Washington

Evergreen Point Bridge

90

The Evergreen Point Bridge

The Evergreen Point Bridge—7,578 feet in length—is the longest floating bridge in the world. It was the second floating bridge built across Lake Washington and was opened in 1963. The lake lies between the coastal city of Seattle, Washington, and the inland part of the state. The first bridge built across the lake was also a floating bridge. After it opened in 1940, travel to Seattle became much easier for people living on the eastern shore of Lake Washington, and the towns there grew in population. Traffic became too heavy for the existing bridge to handle alone. A second floating bridge was planned, to be built south of the first one. It would extend from Seattle to Evergreen Point, near Bellevue. Construction of the Evergreen Point Bridge began in 1960. Almost exactly 3 years later, it was opened to traffic.

The bridge consists of a floating portion that is linked to land on either end by short, ordinary bridges. The floating portion of the bridge is constructed of rectangular concrete sections called pontoons. The pontoons float in a line, partly covered by water, like a boat or barge. Each of the 19 main pontoons is 360 feet long and weighs 4,725 tons. The pontoons are linked by cables to 58 concrete anchors on the lake bottom. Near the center of the floating portion is a drawbridge that opens in an unusual way. Two pontoons back away from each other and withdraw under 2 spans of the bridge, which are lifted more than 7 feet into the air. This creates an opening 200 feet wide through which ships can pass.

Location: Between Seattle, Washington, and the eastern shore of Lake Washington

Type: Pontoon

Body of water spanned: Lake Washington

Opened: August 28, 1963

Length: Floating structure 7,578 feet

Construction time: 3 years

Cost: $34 million

Fun fact: A total of 115,500 vehicles cross over the 4-lane bridge each day.

Opposite page:
The Evergreen Point Bridge was built as a floating bridge because the bottom of Lake Washington was too muddy for a standard bridge.

AMERICA'S TOP
10
BRIDGES

Philadelphia

Pennypack Creek

Upper
Holmsburg

Frankford Avenue

**Frankford
Avenue
Bridge**

Holmsburg

The Frankford Avenue Bridge

★ ★ ★ ★ ★ ★ ★ ★ ★ ★ ★ ★

Some bridges deserve recognition because of their immense size, the great waters they span, or the large numbers of vehicles that cross them. The Frankford Avenue Bridge is small. It crosses a little stream in northeastern Philadelphia. Only about 13,700 vehicles pass over it daily. Even so, in September 1996, a crew filming a documentary for Japanese television on the world's great bridges came to this little stone crossing over Pennypack Creek. They were there because of the age of the Frankford Avenue Bridge—it was built in 1697.

Planning for the bridge began in the 1690s, when a highway called the Great Frankford Road was built between Philadelphia and New York City. Local men provided plenty of help in building the bridge. Anyone who lent a hand did not have to pay taxes.

The Frankford Avenue Bridge is made of stone and is supported by arches. The design of the bridge is ancient, dating back to the Romans. It has 3 spans. Two are 24 feet long and the third is 13 feet long. In 1893, in order to widen and strengthen the bridge so that trolleys could cross it, another bridge was built and attached alongside it. The original bridge is still there, however, and looks almost as it did in 1690.

The Frankford Avenue Bridge was an important crossing during the time of the American Revolution. Troops of the Continental Army marched across it. And in 1789, on April 30, George Washington crossed the bridge as he traveled to New York City for his presidential inauguration.

Location: Philadelphia, Pennsylvania
Type: Stone arch
Body of water spanned: Pennypack Creek
Opened: 1697
Length: Main bridge 61 feet
Fun fact: According to legend, the bridge was placed where it is so that William Penn, founder of Pennsylvania, could reach his summer home outside Philadelphia with ease.

Opposite page:
Philadelphians recently celebrated the 300th anniversary of the Frankford Avenue Bridge.

AMERICA'S TOP

10

BRIDGES

Marin County

101

**Golden
Gate Bridge**

*Golden Gate
Strait*

San Francisco

The
Golden Gate Bridge

★ ★ ★ ★ ★ ★   ★ ★ ★ ★ ★ ★

The Golden Gate Bridge is recognized by the American Society of Civil Engineers as one of the 7 civil engineering wonders of the world. When it opened in 1937, the bridge had the longest main span of any suspension bridge in existence. It held that record until the completion of the Verrazano–Narrows Bridge in 1964. The Golden Gate Bridge links San Francisco, with California's Marin County. It spans Golden Gate, a strait—or narrow water passage—between San Francisco Bay and the Pacific Ocean.

Work on the Golden Gate Bridge began in 1933. Four years later, President Franklin D. Roosevelt announced to the world that the bridge was open by pressing a telegraph key at the White House.

The job of building the bridge, whose towers stand 746 feet above the water, was difficult and dangerous. The Golden Gate Strait is swept by fierce currents and tides. For much of the year, fog cloaks the bay every day. Many safety precautions had to be taken. Workers who had to climb to great heights were put on special diets to prevent dizziness. A huge safety net was slung beneath the bridge. It saved the lives of 19 workers who fell off the bridge. Then, in 1937, on February 17, disaster struck. A scaffold gave way, and broke through the net. Ten men died in the accident.

Work on the 5-lane Golden Gate Bridge continues. In the mid-1990s a project to strengthen it against earthquakes was begun.

Location: Between San Francisco and Marin Counties, California
Type: Suspension
Body of water spanned: Golden Gate Strait
Opened: May 28, 1937
Length: Suspended structure 6,450 feet; main span 4,200 feet
Construction time: 53 months
Cost: $35 million
Fun fact: The bridge has 80,000 miles of wire in its cables.

Opposite page:
The Golden Gate Bridge is a landmark of the San Francisco Bay area.

AMERICA'S TOP

10

BRIDGES

St. Ignace

Straits of
Mackinac

Mackinac Bridge

75

Mackinaw
City

The
Mackinac Bridge

★ ★ ★ ★ ★ ★ ★ ★ ★ ★ ★ ★ ★ ★

The Mackinac Bridge, in Michigan, soars over the Straits of Mackinac (pronounced MACK-in-naw). Its 2 main towers reach 552 feet above the surface of the cold, blue water. The maximum clearance for ships passing under the bridge—many of them huge freighters—is 155 feet. The bridge is noted for its length as well as its height. Its main span is the second-longest in the United States.

The Straits of Mackinac, which link Lake Michigan and Lake Huron, separate southern Michigan from the northern part of the state. The straits are up to 290 feet deep, and during the winter, the surface of the water is whipped by storms and covered with floating ice. It is no wonder that before it opened in 1957, the Mackinac Bridge was called "the bridge that couldn't be built."

Building the steel and concrete structure took more than 3 years. Construction began in the spring of 1954, when workers started on the foundations of the piers that would support the towers. Almost 1 million tons of concrete were poured to make the piers, which stood as much as 210 feet below the water.

The 3,500 workers at the bridge site had to take advantage of the good weather in spring, summer, and early fall. By late fall, storms blasted the Great Lakes region. During the height of the winter, construction was shut down completely. When the Mackinac Bridge was finally opened, the northern and southern parts of Michigan were united by a roadway for the first time.

Location: Between St. Ignace and Mackinaw City, Michigan
Type: Suspension
Body of water spanned: Straits of Mackinac
Opened: November 1, 1957
Length: Suspended structure 8,614 feet; main span 3,800 feet
Construction time: 41 months
Cost: $99.8 million
Fun fact: In order to build the bridge, workers used 4.9 million steel rivets, 1 million steel bolts, and, for the main cables, 42,000 miles of wire.

Opposite page:
The Mackinac Bridge soars above the icy Straits of Mackinac.

AMERICA'S TOP

10

BRIDGES

← Parkdale

Arkansas River

Royal Gorge
Bridge

Royal Gorge

Cañon
City →

The
Royal Gorge Bridge

The Royal Gorge Bridge, in south-central Colorado, is considered the highest suspension bridge in the world. It spans a gorge—a narrow passage with steep, rocky sides—created by the swirling waters of the Arkansas River, 1,053 feet below. Unlike most other bridges, the one spanning Royal Gorge was intended to be a tourist attraction.

The Royal Gorge first attracted major attention in 1877, after silver was discovered at Leadville, to the north. Two railroad companies, the Santa Fe and the Denver & Rio Grande, fought over the right to lay track across the gorge. The courts awarded the rail route to the Denver & Rio Grande Railroad Company.

Traveling by train over the gorge soon became a popular activity. Even President Theodore Roosevelt was a frequent visitor. In 1907, the U.S. Congress turned the gorge over to Cañon City for a municipal park.

During the 1920s, a Texan named Lon Piper received permission to build a bridge over the gorge and operate it as a tourist attraction. Construction of the bridge began in June 1929 and was finished in only 6 months. The first step was to pour a concrete abutment on each rim of the canyon to support the ends of the bridge. Then 2 towers were erected. Next, two 300-ton cables were stretched between the towers and to each abutment.

The bridge is now part of an amusement complex. Since it was first opened, millions of people have crossed the bridge on foot, in automobiles, and on a trolley.

Location: 8 miles west of Cañon City, Colorado
Type: Suspension
Body of water spanned: Arkansas River
Opened: December 6, 1929
Length: Suspended structure 1,260 feet; main span 938 feet
Construction time: 6 months
Cost: $350,000
Fun fact: Even though most of the workers who built the bridge were local men with no experience, there were no major accidents.

Opposite page:
The Royal Gorge Bridge spans the Arkansas River, 1,053 feet below.

AMERICA'S TOP

10

BRIDGES

San Francisco–
Oakland Bay
Bridge

80

Oakland

San
Francisco   San Francisco Bay

The
San Francisco–Oakland Bay Bridge

★ ★ ★ ★ ★ ★   ★ ★ ★ ★ ★ ★

The American Society of Civil Engineers has designated the San Francisco–Oakland Bay Bridge a National Historic Civil Engineering Landmark. The structure is actually 3 bridges— 2 suspension bridges and 1 cantilever bridge.

The construction of the bridge, which began in July 1933, was an immense and difficult job. This was partly because of the width of the bay, which is about 5 miles. Water depth was also a problem. Concrete for the piers supporting the bridge was poured to a depth of 218 feet, 33 feet deeper than concrete had ever been poured.

The 2 suspension bridges were built over the western part of San Francisco Bay that is 2 miles wide. They were connected by a huge "island" of concrete. The suspension bridges were extended to Yerba Buena Island, in the middle of the bay. There, engineers designed a tunnel that connected it to the cantilever bridge on the Oakland side. Construction of the bridge began in 1933 and was finished in the fall of 1936, six months ahead of schedule. While building the bridge, workers pulled up a large tooth of a prehistoric mammoth, which had been at the bottom of the bay! The bridge was officially opened by President Franklin D. Roosevelt, who pressed a button in Washington that turned on a green "go" signal light. At the signal, 3 columns of automobiles started over the bridge.

Part of the bridge collapsed during the earthquake of October 1989, and was repaired and reopened the next month. Now, about 275,000 vehicles per day travel over the bridge's 2 levels.

Location: Between Oakland and San Francisco, California
Type: Suspension; cantilever
Body of water spanned: San Francisco Bay
Opened: November 12, 1936
Length: Suspension 2,310 feet; cantilever 10,176 feet
Construction time: 40 months
Cost: $77 million
Fun fact: During peak traffic, 9,000 vehicles per hour cross the bridge.

Opposite page:
The San Francisco–Oakland Bay Bridge spans the 5-mile width of San Francisco Bay.

AMERICA'S TOP

10

BRIDGES

The Narrows

278

Brooklyn

Staten Island

**Verrazano–
Narrows Bridge**

Atlantic Ocean

The
Verrazano–Narrows Bridge

The Verrazano–Narrows Bridge, in New York City, has the longest main span of any suspension bridge in North America. It is huge, with 2 towers that are 693 feet above the average high water level. The piers that support the towers reach down to a depth of 170 feet below the average high tide. Each massive tower weighs 27,000 tons and is held together by 3 million steel rivets and 1 million steel bolts.

The bridge is named after the Italian navigator Giovanni da Verrazano, the first European to sail into New York harbor. He entered the harbor in 1524 through a channel between Lower and Upper New York Bays. Today, this channel is called the Narrows.

The bridge has 2 levels, crossed by more than 60 million vehicles per year, traveling between the boroughs of Brooklyn and Staten Island. Each of the 4 cables that supports the bridge is almost 39 inches in diameter. And each cable contains a total of 26,108 steel wires. Together, the anchorages required more than 375,000 cubic yards of concrete. The base of each anchorage is 230 feet wide and 345 feet long, about the total area of 2 football fields placed alongside each other!

Great ships from around the world pass through the Narrows on their way to New York harbor. The largest of these pass easily under the immense Verrazano–Narrows Bridge. During an average tide, there is 228 feet of room between the bridge and the water.

Location: Between Staten Island and Brooklyn, in New York City
Type: Suspension
Body of water spanned: The Narrows
Opened: Upper level November 21, 1964; lower level June 28, 1969
Length: Suspended structure 6,690 feet; main span 4,260 feet
Construction time: 63 months
Cost: $320.1 million
Fun fact: The roadway of the Verrazano is 12 feet lower in summer—when the metal in the bridge expands—than in winter—when the metal contracts.

Opposite page:
The Verrazano–Narrows Bridge has the longest span of any North American bridge.

America's Top 10 Bridges are not necessarily the longest. Although length was a basis for inclusion, we also considered a bridge's historical significance and the challenges that it presented to engineers when it was built. Below are 10 additional important bridges.

More American Bridges			
Bridge	Type	Location	Main Span
Bayonne	steel arch	New Jersey	1,652 feet
Bronx-Whitestone	suspension	New York	2,300 feet
Comodore Barry	cantilever	Pennsylvania	1,622 feet
Columbia River	continuous truss	Washington–Oregon	1,232 feet
Francis Scott Key	continuous truss	Maryland	1,200 feet
George Washington	suspension	New York–New Jersey	3,500 feet
Mississippi River	cantilever	Louisiana	1,575 feet
Newport	suspension	Rhode Island	1,600 feet
Ravenswood	cantilever	West Virginia	1,723 feet
Tacoma Narrows	suspension	Washington	2,800 feet

Newport Bridge

See page 228 for more information about bridges.

AMERICA'S TOP

10

CITIES

AMERICA'S TOP

10

CITIES

Chicago

★ ★ ★ ★ ★ ★ ★ ★ ★ ★ ★ ★ ★ ★ ★ ★ ★

Chicago is located on the southwestern shore of Lake Michigan. It is the only inland city in the country that is connected by water to both the Atlantic Ocean and the Gulf of Mexico. Chicago's location has made it an important transportation center since the early 1800s. Many highways and railroad routes meet in Chicago, and it has 3 airports—including O'Hare International Airport, the busiest airport in the world. The city was founded by Jean Baptiste Point du Sable, a fur trader, in 1779.

Chicago is famous for its spectacular architecture. The world's first skyscraper, the Home Insurance Company, was built there in 1885. It was 9 stories tall. Today, 3 of the world's 10 tallest buildings are in Chicago: the Sears Tower (the tallest building in America), the Amoco Building, and the John Hancock Center.

The central business area is called the Loop. Originally, this area was within a loop of elevated train tracks. North of the Loop is the Chicago River. Its flow was reversed by engineers in 1900 to prevent industrial wastes from flowing into Lake Michigan. It is the only river in the world that flows backward! Every year on St. Patrick's Day, the Chicago River is dyed green.

For much of the last century, Chicago has been known for its stockyards and meat-processing plants, and today, food processing is still a leading industry. For example, Chicago is home to the Nabisco Biscuit Company, the world's largest cookie and cracker factory, where 16 billion Oreo cookies are made each year.

Name: From the Potawatomi name, Checaugou, meaning "place of the wild onion"
Nickname: Windy City
Location: Illinois
Incorporated: 1837
Population and rank: 2.7 million; 3rd largest
Size: 228 square miles
Elevation: 623 feet
Important industries: Financial services, food processing, manufacturing, transportation, wholesale and retail trade
Landmarks: Amoco Building, Buckingham Fountain, John Hancock Center, Sears Tower
Tallest building: Sears Tower (110 stories)
Sports teams: Cubs, White Sox (baseball); Bears (football); Bulls (basketball); BlackHawks (hockey)
Fun fact: The first zippers were made here in 1896.

Opposite page:
Chicago is home to 3 of the world's tallest buildings, including the John Hancock Center (black building).

AMERICA'S TOP

10

CITIES

Dallas

★ ★ ★ ★ ★ ★ ★ ★ ★ ★ ★ ★ ★ ★ ★ ★ ★

Dallas is an important manufacturing center. Airplane parts, electronic equipment, processed foods, machinery, and clothing are all made there. The city also is a major financial and commercial center. Each year, hundreds of thousands of people go to Dallas to buy merchandise for their stores and businesses. Most of them arrive by plane, landing at DFW International Airport, the world's third-busiest airport. DFW takes up more space than New York's island of Manhattan!

The city was founded in 1841, when John Neely Bryan opened a trading post on the banks of the Trinity River. Bryan sketched out a town, including a courthouse square and 20 streets. Settlers came, and gradually the city grew. Today, it is America's ninth-largest city, filled with tall, modern buildings. Dallas's past is still remembered, however. In Historical Plaza is the small log cabin built by Bryan more than 150 years ago. Nearby, in Pioneer Plaza, is a sculpture of larger-than-life bronze longhorn steers and cowboys on horseback. These figures are located on an actual cattle trail that was used in the 1800s.

One of the city's most popular events is the state fair, held each fall. The largest state fair in America, it opens with a parade downtown. Most of the activities take place in Fair Park, where many of the buildings date back to the Texas Centennial Exposition—the 6-month 100th birthday party for the state. These buildings form the oldest world's fair site in the United States. Another park landmark is Cotton Bowl Stadium, where football games and other events are held.

Name: There are several explanations. The name may honor George Mifflin Dallas, vice president of the United States in 1846.
Nickname: Big D
Location: Texas
Incorporated: 1856
Population and rank: 1.1 million; 9th largest
Size: 378 square miles
Elevation: 450 to 750 feet
Important industries: Commerce, finance, manufacturing, transportation
Landmarks: Fair Park, Historical Plaza, Pioneer Plaza
Tallest building: NationsBank (72 stories)
Sports teams: Rangers (baseball), Cowboys (football), Mavericks (basketball), Stars (hockey), Sidekicks (indoor soccer)
Fun fact: The Tex-Mex dish chicken fajitas was invented here.

Opposite page:
The modern Dallas skyline mixes with the city's pioneer past.

AMERICA'S TOP
10
CITIES

Detroit

★ ★ ★ ★ ★ ★ ★ ★ ★ ★ ★ ★ ★ ★ ★ ★

Detroit is often called Motor City—or Motown, for short. Henry Ford began his Ford Motor Company in Detroit in 1903. Soon, Walter Chrysler and Ransom Olds also built automobile plants there. Since that time, the city has been the center of America's automotive industry. About 20 percent of the nation's cars, trucks, and tractors are manufactured in Detroit and the surrounding towns. The city is also home to the world's largest market for small, flowering garden plants.

Detroit was founded in 1701 by a Frenchman named Antoine de la Mothe Cadillac. He established a fur trading post on the west bank of what became known as the Detroit River. The trading post grew into Detroit, America's 10th largest city.

Soaring high into the sky in downtown Detroit is the Renaissance Center. This building complex has 6 office towers, a hotel, and dozens of stores and restaurants. An elevated train, known as the People Mover, connects downtown sites.

Among Detroit's tourist attractions are mansions that automakers built. Meadow Brook Hall was built by John Dodge in the late 1920s. It has 100 rooms and 39 brick chimneys. On the grounds is Knole Cottage, with miniature rooms two-thirds normal size. It was built for Dodge's 12-year-old daughter and was the first all-electric home in Detroit!

Belle Isle, an island in the city, is a popular park for picnics, fishing, baseball, and racquetball. The nation's oldest freshwater aquarium is also located there.

Name: From French words meaning "the straits"
Nicknames: Motor City, Motown, Motor Capital of the World
Location: Michigan
Incorporated: 1802
Population and rank: 1,000,272; 10th largest
Size: 137 square miles
Elevation: 600 feet
Important industries: Automobile manufacturing and trade, shipping
Landmarks: Belle Isle, Meadow Brook Hall, Renaissance Center
Tallest building: Westin Hotel (73 stories)
Sports teams: Tigers (baseball), Lions (football), Pistons (basketball), Red Wings (hockey)
Fun fact: The world's first concrete road was built here.

Opposite page:
The lights of downtown Detroit glisten along the Detroit River.

AMERICA'S TOP
10
CITIES

Houston

★ ★ ★ ★ ★ ★ ★ ★ ★ ★ ★ ★ ★ ★ ★ ★ ★ ★ ★

Houston is the largest city in Texas. It is one of the nation's busiest ports and is the center of America's petroleum industry. Houston is also known for its aerospace industry. The Johnson Space Center designs space missions, trains astronauts, and acts as mission control during flights. At the Space Center, visitors of all ages can direct a space shuttle and space station.

Houston was founded in 1836 by Augustus and John Allen. After sailing up from the Gulf of Mexico, the explorers hired Gail Borden—the inventor of condensed milk—to create a map for the city. The Allens named it after General Samuel Houston, who earlier that year led the Texas army to victory over Mexican forces, gaining independence for Texas.

Some of the city's original buildings still stand, including Kennedy Bakery, built in 1861. In addition to being a bakery, this building also served as an arsenal and a trading post. In Sam Houston Park, the San Jacinto Monument marks the victorious battle for Texas independence.

In the early 1900s, the Houston Ship Channel was created. This 50-mile-long waterway made it possible for large ocean-going ships to travel between Houston and the Gulf of Mexico.

Twenty feet below Houston's downtown is the nation's largest tunnel system. Located in the 6 miles of tunnels are shops and more than 100 restaurants. Just outside the downtown area is the world-famous Astrodome, the world's first domed stadium. It is home to several professional sports teams and the world's largest rodeo.

Name: Honors Samuel Houston, a hero of the Texas war for independence from Mexico
Nicknames: Space City, Bayou City
Location: Texas
Incorporated: 1836
Population and rank: 1.7 million; 4th largest
Size: 573 square miles
Elevation: 49 feet
Important industries: Aerospace, biotechnology, chemicals, oil refining, shipping
Landmarks: Astrodome, Hermann Park, Johnson Space Center, San Jacinto Monument
Tallest building: Transco Tower (64 stories)
Sports teams: Astros (baseball), Oilers (football), Rockets (basketball), Aeros (hockey), Hotshots (indoor soccer)
Fun fact: Home of the world's first domed stadium

Opposite page:
Underneath Houston's skyscrapers lies America's largest tunnel system.

America's Top

10

CITIES

Los Angeles

★ ★ ★ ★ ★ ★ ★ ★ ★ ★ ★ ★ ★ ★ ★ ★ ★ ★

Often called by its initials—L.A.—Los Angeles is located in sunny southern California. Hollywood, which is part of L.A., has made the city America's entertainment capital. It is a famous center for the motion picture, television, radio, and music-recording industries.

Los Angeles is bordered by the Pacific Ocean to the west and south. To the north and east are mountains. The city was established in 1781, when 44 settlers from Mexico made their homes in what is now the downtown area. It remained a small community until the gold rush of 1849, which brought more settlers. Today, Los Angeles is America's second-largest city. Because it is spread out over a large area, almost everyone travels by car. The city is famous for its system of 6- and 8-lane freeways, or highways.

The city's government and financial centers are located downtown. There, too, are ethnic communities such as Chinatown and Little Tokyo. In Hancock Park are the famous La Brea Tar Pits. Thousands of years ago, oil seeped up from deep within the ground, forming pools on the surface. Animals became trapped in the sticky pools and died. The remains of these animals tell us that camels, mastodons, and saber-tooth tigers once lived in southern California.

Hollywood is north of downtown L.A. Along its sidewalks is the Walk of Fame, where colorful stones display the names of celebrities. Handprints and footprints of movie stars are embedded in cement in the famous courtyard of Mann's Chinese Theater (a movie theater).

Name: Originally El Pueblo de Nuestra Señora de los Angeles de Porciuncula ("The Village of Our Lady of the Angels")
Nicknames: L.A., City of Angels
Location: California
Incorporated: 1781
Population and rank: 3.5 million; 2nd largest
Size: 467 square miles
Elevation: 104 feet
Important industries: Health services, international trade, motion pictures, television, tourism
Landmarks: Hollywood Walk of Fame, La Brea Tar Pits
Tallest building: First Interstate World Center (73 stories)
Sports teams: Dodgers (baseball), Clippers, Lakers (basketball), Kings (hockey)
Fun fact: More than 100 tons of fossilized animal bones have been unearthed from La Brea Tar Pits.

Opposite page:
Los Angeles is the center of America's entertainment industry.

New York

★ ★ ★ ★ ★ ★ ★ ★ ★ ★ ★ ★ ★ ★ ★ ★ ★ ★

Popularly known as "the Big Apple," New York is America's largest city. More than 7 million people live there. Each year, the city attracts more than 30 million visitors from all over the globe. Many enjoy Broadway theater productions, visit art museums and galleries, or attend music or dance concerts. The city is considered to be one of the cultural centers of the world.

New York is located on the mouth of the Hudson River, where the river flows into the Atlantic Ocean. The city is divided into 5 counties, called boroughs. Only the Bronx is on the mainland. Staten Island and Manhattan are islands. Brooklyn and Queens are part of Long Island.

Manhattan is the smallest borough, but it is the best known. It is home to many famous buildings, including the Empire State Building, World Trade Center, and United Nations headquarters, where many nations have offices.

The city is filled with well-known landmarks. On a small island in the harbor is the Statue of Liberty, a gift from France to celebrate America's first 100 years of independence. Near the statue is Ellis Island, where millions of immigrants first entered the United States.

New York was America's first capital. A statue of George Washington in front of Federal Hall marks the spot where, in 1789, Washington took the oath of office as the first president of the United States. The hall is in lower Manhattan. At the northern end of the borough is Dyckman House, built around 1783. It is the only remaining farmhouse in Manhattan.

Name: Honors England's Duke of York, who later became King James II of England
Nickname: The Big Apple
Location: New York
Incorporated: 1625, as New Amsterdam
Population and rank: 7.4 million; largest
Size: 301 square miles
Elevation: Sea level to 409 feet
Important industries: Advertising, banking, fashion, financial services, publishing
Landmarks: Central Park, Empire State Building, Statue of Liberty, United Nations, World Trade Center
Tallest buildings: World Trade Towers (110 stories)
Sports teams: Mets, Yankees (baseball), Giants, Jets (football), Knicks (basketball), Islanders, Rangers (hockey)
Fun fact: The hot dog was invented here in 1900.

Opposite page:
The Manhattan skyline rises high above the East River.

Philadelphia

★ ★ ★ ★ ★ ★ ★ ★ ★ ★ ★ ★ ★ ★ ★ ★ ★ ★ ★

Located between the Delaware and Schuylkill Rivers in southeastern Pennsylvania, Philadelphia is one of the largest cities on the East Coast. The city was founded in 1682 by William Penn, an English Quaker who wanted it to be a center of religious freedom. During Colonial days, it was America's largest city. From 1790 to 1800 it was also the nation's capital.

Philadelphia is brimming with historic sites. At Independence National Historical Park is Independence Hall, where America's founders adopted the Declaration of Independence on July 4, 1776. The Liberty Bell, which was rung when the declaration was approved, is nearby. So is Carpenters Hall, where the First Continental Congress met in 1774. Today, visitors to the City Tavern can sit in the same spot where George Washington, Benjamin Franklin, and other Colonial leaders sat more than 200 years ago!

Philadelphia's first commercial area, near the waterfront, is known as Old City. The Betsy Ross House is there. According to legend, this is where Ross created the first American flag.

Along the Delaware River is a park called Penn's Landing. Historic ships, including the U.S.S. *Olympia* from the Spanish-American War, are docked there, and numerous festivals are held in the park. Philadelphia's port has been important since Colonial days. Each year, millions of tons of cargo flow through its facilities.

On the city's west side is Fairmount Park. It has more than 8,900 acres of meadows, trails, winding creeks, and the Philadelphia Zoo.

Name: Philadelphia comes from the Greek words for "brotherly love."

Nicknames: Philly, City of Brotherly Love

Location: Pennsylvania

Incorporated: 1682

Population and rank: 1.5 million; 5th largest

Size: 129 square miles

Elevation: 5 to 150 feet

Important industries: Health care, oil refining, petroleum products, pharmaceuticals, shipping

Landmarks: Fairmount Park, Independence Hall, Liberty Bell, Old City

Tallest building: Liberty Place (61 stories)

Sports teams: Phillies (baseball), Eagles (football), 76ers (basketball), Flyers (hockey)

Fun fact: The nation's first daily newspaper was published here.

Opposite page:
Philadelphia's skyline is a mix of old and new.

AMERICA'S TOP
10
CITIES

Phoenix

Phoenix, the capital of Arizona, is the state's largest city. Because of its dry, sunny climate, Phoenix is a major resort center. It is also known for its high-tech and aerospace industries.

Phoenix is located along the banks of the Salt River, in the Valley of the Sun. This valley is the northern tip of the Sonoran Desert and is bordered by dramatic mountain ranges.

Many centuries ago, Native Americans known as the Hohokams lived there. They built canals from the Salt River to water their fields. For unknown reasons, the Hohokams disappeared around the year 1450. In 1865, the U.S. Army established a fort in the nearby mountains. In 1870, Phoenix was created along the lines of the ancient Hohokam canals. It had only 300 inhabitants but grew steadily. Today, many people move to Phoenix for the pleasant climate.

The city's best-known landmark is Camelback Mountain, named for its camel-like profile. Another landmark is Tovrea Castle, which was built by a wealthy cattle rancher.

South Mountain Park—the world's largest city park—covers more than 20,000 acres. More than 300 kinds of plants live there, as well as coyotes, foxes, rabbits, lizards, and many other animals. A short distance to the north of the park is the Desert Botanical Garden, which displays one of the world's best collections of desert plants.

The state capitol building was built in 1900. It was made from local materials, including stone quarried from Camelback Mountain and copper from Arizona's famous copper mines.

Name: Refers to the mythical bird that rose from its own ashes, just as the city grew from the ruins of the Hohokam civilization.
Nickname: Valley of the Sun
Location: Arizona
Incorporated: 1881
Population and rank: 1.2 million; 7th largest
Size: 450 square miles
Elevation: 1,117 feet
Important industries: Aerospace, construction, high-tech industry, tourism
Landmarks: Camelback Mountain, Heritage Square, South Mountain Park, Tovrea Castle
Tallest building: Bank One Building (40 stories)
Sports teams: Cardinals (football), Suns (basketball), Coyotes (hockey)
Fun fact: The Phoenix Zoo is credited with saving the Arabian oryx—a type of antelope—from extinction.

Opposite page:
Phoenix is the largest city in Arizona.

AMERICA'S TOP
10
CITIES

San Antonio

$\star$ $\star$ $\star$ $\star$ $\star$ $\star$ $\star$ $\star$ $\star$ $\star$ $\star$ $\star$ $\star$ $\star$ $\star$ $\star$ $\star$ $\star$

San Antonio is one of America's largest cities, and an important commercial and industrial center. The city's beginning dates back to 1691, when a group of Spanish explorers came upon a river in south-central Texas. It was the feast day of Saint Anthony, so they named the river San Antonio in his honor. In 1718, Spaniards founded a military post on the banks of the river. They also established a mission (church and fort) nearby called the Alamo. The fort became famous in 1836. For 13 days, 189 Texans held the fort against some 4,000 Mexican troops. The Texans lost the battle, but "Remember the Alamo!" became the motto of the Texas war for independence.

The Alamo and 4 other Spanish missions built in the early 1700s are among the many historic structures in the city that have been lovingly preserved. The Spanish Governor's Palace was built in 1749. Across the street is Navarro House, the home of one of the leaders of the Texas Revolution. These historic sites are museums that provide glimpses of what life was like long ago.

Some of San Antonio's old buildings have been put to new uses. One from the 1850s is the city's Cowboy Museum. Others are found in Market Square—the largest Mexican marketplace outside of Mexico.

The San Antonio River still winds through the center of the city. Along its banks is the popular Paseo del Rio, better known as River Walk. Every year, the Fiesta River Parade and the Holiday River Parade float down the river on barges.

Name: Honors the Catholic saint, San Antonio de Padua (St. Anthony of Padua)

Nicknames: Alamo City, Cradle of Texas Liberty

Location: Texas

Incorporated: 1837

Population and rank: 1.1 million; 8th largest

Size: 377 square miles

Elevation: 701 feet

Important industries: Medical, retail trade, tourism, wholesale

Landmarks: Alamo, River Walk, Spanish Governor's Palace, Spanish missions

Tallest building: Tower of the Americas (59 stories)

Sports teams: Spurs (basketball), Iguanas (hockey)

Fun fact: The first canned chili con carne and tamales were produced here in 1911.

Opposite page:
Among San Antonio's modern skyscrapers lie many historic buildings.

AMERICA'S TOP

10

CITIES

★ ★ ★ ★ ★ ★ ★ ★ ★ ★ ★ ★ ★ ★ ★ ★ ★

San Diego

San Diego lies on the Pacific Ocean in the southwest corner of California, close to the Mexican border. It is an important center of trade for the southwestern United States and for northern Mexico. It also is an important manufacturing center, particularly for the aerospace and electronics industries. A large sport-fishing fleet and a U.S. Navy base are located there as well.

San Diego is known as the birthplace of California. In 1542, explorer Juan Rodriguez Cabrillo became the first European to discover California. He sailed north from Mexico and landed in what is now San Diego Bay. In 1769, Spanish missionaries founded Mission San Diego de Alcala with the hope of converting Native Americans to Christianity. It was the first mission in California. During the same period of time, the Spanish established a base there for exploring California. This base slowly grew into one of America's largest cities. Much of the original settlement can still be seen in Old Town, and there are historic buildings in the Gaslamp Quarter, too. The quarter is surrounded by modern skyscrapers with mirror-like exteriors that appear silver, bronze, or black.

The city's most famous and most popular attraction is the San Diego Zoo, which is home to more than 3,900 animals. Many of the animals are housed in beautifully constructed natural habitats, such as Hippo Beach, Polar Bear Plunge, and Tiger River. There is also a petting zoo, a baby animal nursery, and large enclosures filled with colorful birds.

Name: Honors San Diego de Alcala de Henares (St. James of Alcala)
Nickname: Birthplace of California
Location: California
Incorporated: 1850
Population and rank: 1.2 million; 6th largest
Size: 320 square miles
Elevation: Sea level to 1,591 feet
Important industries: Electronics, government, high-tech, tourism
Landmarks: Cabrillo National Monument, Old Town, San Diego Zoo
Tallest building: Hyatt Regency San Diego (40 stories)
Sports teams: Padres (baseball), Chargers (football), Sockers (indoor soccer)
Fun fact: The first drive-through restaurant, a Jack-in-the-Box, opened here in 1951.

Opposite page:
San Diego's skyline sparkles against the deep blue Pacific Ocean.

America's Top 10 Cities are not necessarily the "best" cities, but they have the largest populations, according to 1996 U.S. Census figures. Below is a list of the capitals and the largest cities in each state.

America's Capitals and Largest Cities

State, Capital,
Largest City, Population

Alabama, Montgomery,
Birmingham, 258,543

Alaska, Juneau,
Anchorage, 250,505

Arizona, Phoenix,
Phoenix, 1,159,014

Arkansas, Little Rock,
Little Rock, 175,752

California, Sacramento,
Los Angeles, 3,553,638

Colorado, Denver,
Denver, 497,840

Connecticut, Hartford,
Bridgeport, 134,996

Delaware, Dover,
Wilmington, 69,490

Florida, Tallahassee,
Jacksonville, 679,792

Georgia, Atlanta,
Atlanta, 401,907

Hawaii, Honolulu,
Honolulu, 423,475

Idaho, Boise,
Boise, 152,737

Illinois, Springfield,
Chicago, 2,721,547

Indiana, Indianapolis,
Indianapolis, 746,737

Iowa, Des Moines,
Des Moines, 193,422

Kansas, Topeka,
Wichita, 320,395

Kentucky, Frankfort,
Louisville, 260,689

Louisiana, Baton Rouge,
New Orleans, 476,625

Maine, Augusta,
Portland, 69,803

Maryland, Annapolis,
Baltimore, 675,401

Massachusetts, Boston,
Boston, 558,394

Michigan, Lansing,
Detroit, 1,000,272

Minnesota, St. Paul,
Minneapolis, 358,785

Mississippi, Jackson,
Jackson, 192,923

Missouri, Jefferson City,
Kansas City, 441,259

Montana, Helena,
Billings, 103,419

Nebraska, Lincoln,
Omaha, 364,253

Nevada, Carson City,
Las Vegas, 376,906

New Hampshire, Concord,
Manchester, 100,967

New Jersey, Trenton,
Newark, 268,510

New Mexico, Santa Fe,
Albuquerque, 419,681

New York, Albany,
New York City, 7,380,906

North Carolina, Raleigh,
Charlotte, 441,297

North Dakota, Bismarck,
Fargo, 53,514

Ohio, Columbus,
Columbus, 657,053

Oklahoma, Oklahoma City,
Oklahoma City, 469,852

Oregon, Salem,
Portland, 480,824

Pennsylvania, Harrisburg,
Philadelphia, 1,478,002

Rhode Island, Providence,
Providence, 152,558

South Carolina, Columbia,
Columbia, 112,773

South Dakota, Pierre,
Sioux Falls, 116,506

Tennessee, Nashville,
Memphis, 596,725

Texas, Austin,
Houston, 1,744,058

Utah, Salt Lake City,
Salt Lake City, 172,575

Vermont, Montpelier,
Burlington, 40,262

Virginia, Richmond,
Virginia Beach, 430,385

Washington, Olympia,
Seattle, 524,704

West Virginia, Charleston,
Charleston, 60,694

Wisconsin, Madison,
Milwaukee, 590,503

Wyoming, Cheyenne,
Cheyenne, 59,583

See page 228 for more information about cities.

AMERICA'S TOP

10

CONSTRUCTION WONDERS

AMERICA'S TOP

10

CONSTRUCTION WONDERS

AK

CANADA

Alaska Pipeline

The Alaska Pipeline

The 800-mile-long Alaska Pipeline carries oil across the entire length of the state. It crosses steep mountains, raging rivers, and permafrost— a permanently frozen layer beneath the earth's surface. The line was constructed by the Alyeska Pipeline Service Company and was an extremely complicated building project.

In 1968, oil was found under the ground in Prudhoe Bay, on Alaska's northern coast. The pipeline was built to carry the oil from Prudhoe Bay to the port of Valdez. There, large ships would pick up the crude oil and take it to refineries in the "Lower 48" states.

Alyeska's first major construction problem involved crossing Alaska's permafrost. The heat from the pipeline could thaw the frozen ground, so Alyeska's engineers decided to elevate the pipeline where necessary. Special crossings were built so that the migration routes of native caribou would not be disturbed.

The pipe itself is 48 inches in diameter, and it is wrapped with 4 inches of insulation. The sections that did not need to be elevated were buried between 3 and 35 feet below ground. In addition to the pipeline, 10 pumping stations were built to keep the oil moving.

In 1977, on August 1, the first tanker left Valdez carrying oil that had been transported through the Alaska Pipeline. Over a million barrels flow through the pipeline every day. Since oil is a limited natural resource, we will eventually use up the oil in Alaska. Today, the search for new sources of oil continues.

Location: Alaska
Completed: June 1977
Length: 800 miles
Diameter of pipe: 48 inches
Amount of oil flowing through pipeline: 1.6 million barrels per day
Cost: $8 billion
Fun fact: More than 83,000 sections of pipe were welded together to make the pipeline.

Opposite page:
The Alaska Pipeline was built in a zigzag pattern, which helps the pipeline adjust to the changing temperature of the oil.

AMERICA'S TOP

10

CONSTRUCTION WONDERS

AL   GA

Atlantic
Ocean

FL

Epcot
Center

Gulf of Mexico

Epcot Center

★ ★ ★ ★ ★ ★ ★ ★ ★ ★ ★ ★ ★ ★ ★ ★ ★ ★

On October 1, in 1982, the Experimental Prototype Community of Tomorrow (Epcot Center) opened at Disney World in Florida. Walt Disney, who produced many famous animated cartoons, had the idea for Epcot Center in 1966. He wanted people to think about how science affects the future, and he wanted them to appreciate the many cultures of the world. The 2 main parts of Epcot Center—Future World and World Showcase—demonstrate these ideas.

Construction began in October 1979. To build Epcot Center, workers moved 54 million tons of earth, and they used 16,000 tons of steel and 500,000 feet of lumber! The total cost of the project was $900 million.

Spaceship Earth, which is located at the entrance to Epcot Center, is one of the most amazing engineering feats at Disney World. It is built like a geodesic dome—a strong, dome-like structure that has a framework of triangular shapes. Spaceship Earth is a sphere, however, instead of a half-circle. It is the world's first geodesic sphere and the largest geodesic structure. The sphere weighs 15.5 million pounds. It is 180 feet high and 165 feet in diameter. There are 954 triangular panels that form the outside of the structure. It is supported by 6 steel legs that are sunk 100 feet into the ground. Inside, visitors to Spaceship Earth ride on a motorized track that winds around the sphere. Along the way, passengers view exhibits relating to the history of communications—from the first printing press to astronauts' communications from space.

Location: Florida
Opened: October 1, 1982
Area: 260 acres
Cost: $900 million
Fun fact: About 10,000 workers helped build Spaceship Earth.

Opposite page:
Spaceship Earth is the world's largest geodesic building.

AMERICA'S TOP 10 CONSTRUCTION WONDERS

CANADA
ME
VT
NH
Erie Canal
MA
NY
RI
CT
PA
NJ

The Erie Canal

Building the Erie Canal—the longest canal in America—was an amazing accomplishment at a time when construction equipment was much less advanced than it is today. In the early 1800s, transporting people and goods was difficult. In order to travel westward from the East Coast, people had to cross the Appalachian Mountains, which run from Maine to Georgia. In 1807, a man named Jesse Hawley had the idea of building a canal, or human-made waterway. This would connect the Hudson River to Lake Erie—a distance of 363 miles! Westward travel, he said, would be easier by boat than by land.

In 1817, on July 4, a groundbreaking ceremony was held in Rome, New York. It took workers the next 8 years to complete the Erie Canal. Many obstacles, such as rocky ridges, huge trees, and muddy swamps, stood in the way.

Structures called "locks" were built to allow boats to be raised or lowered between sections of the canal that varied in depth. The double locks that raised and lowered boats over a 76-foot-high ridge in Lockport, New York, were especially impressive. In some places the canal had to be elevated above ground level. To solve this problem, engineers designed aqueducts—raised structures designed to carry water.

In 1820, a passenger boat traveled through the first completed section of the canal. Five and a half years later, on October 26 in 1825, the entire canal was open. It was a huge success. By 1836, more than 3,000 boats traveled back and forth regularly on the canal.

Location: New York State
Opened: October 26, 1825
Length: 363 miles
Width: 40 feet at top; 28 feet at bottom
Depth: 4 feet
Number of locks: 83
Number of aqueducts: 18
Cost: More than $7 million
Fun fact: To announce the departure of the first boat on the canal, cannons were fired along the length of the canal and down the Hudson River to New York City.

Opposite page:
A boat motors down the tree-lined Erie Canal.

AMERICA'S TOP
10
CONSTRUCTION WONDERS

NE IA

KS

Gateway Arch
MO

IL

OK AR

KY

TN

The Gateway Arch

★ ★ ★ ★ ★ ★ ★ ★ ★ ★ ★ ★ ★ ★

In the 1930s, a St. Louis lawyer named Luther Ely Smith had the idea of building a memorial to commemorate St. Louis's role as a gateway to the West in the 1800s. Because of money problems and World War II, however, it took 30 years for the Gateway Arch to be completed.

After the war, in 1947, a contest was held to design the memorial, which was won by the architect Eero Saarinen. To symbolize a gateway, he designed a steel arch in the shape of an upside-down catenary—the curve that is made by a chain when it is suspended loosely between 2 points.

For the foundation, about 26,000 tons of concrete were poured into two 60-foot-deep holes, and 252 steel supports were set into the concrete. Once the foundation was ready, sections of the steel arch were lifted by crane and put in place, one at a time. When the 2 legs of the arch reached 72 feet, special rigs called "creeper derricks" were made for each leg. They carried the cranes on platforms high into the air.

On October 28, in 1965, a crowd of people cheered as the last steel section of the arch was placed. A "tram" elevator was installed to take visitors to the top. Because of the curved shape of the arch, the tram had free-swinging compartments, much like the seats on a Ferris wheel!

Once the arch was completed, work began on the underground visitors center. The Gateway Arch was dedicated on May 25 in 1968. Its official name is the Jefferson National Expansion Memorial in honor of United States president Thomas Jefferson.

Location: St. Louis, Missouri
Dedicated: May 25, 1968
Height: 630 feet
Weight: More than 16,000 tons
Designer: Eero Saarinen
Number of visitors:
 4.5 million per year
Cost: $13 million
Fun fact: When the Mississippi River flooded in 1993, workers pumped more than 1,000 gallons of water per minute out of the visitors center.

Opposite page:
The graceful form of the Gateway Arch is reflected in the Mississippi River.

AMERICA'S TOP

10

CONSTRUCTION WONDERS

CANADA

WA   ★ Grand
           Coulee
           Dam

OR   ID

The Grand Coulee Dam

★ ★ ★ ★ ★ ★ ★ ★   ★ ★ ★ ★ ★ ★ ★ ★

The Grand Coulee Dam, in the state of Washington, is the largest producer of hydro-electricity in America and third-largest in the world. When it was begun, it was the largest concrete structure ever built. About 12 million cubic yards of concrete were used to construct the dam—enough concrete to build a sidewalk that circles the earth twice!

In 1933, on July 16, a crowd of 3,000 people watched as the first stake was driven into the site of the Grand Coulee Dam. The dam, which was built in 2 parts, uses the Columbia River as a source of electric power. The dam also irrigates the dry farmlands of the region.

Before the dam could be built, it was necessary to uncover the underlying rock for the foundation. Shovel operators scooped up 20,000 wheelbarrow-loads of dirt every 7 hours, dumping it onto the largest conveyor system ever made. This "river of dirt" traveled 1 mile to what is now Crescent Bay Lake.

In December 1935, the first concrete was poured. Once the base was finished, the dam's steel skeleton was built. More than 20,000 interlocking concrete columns were then installed. By December 1941, the spillway—the area where water flows down a vast wall—was completed. Two power plants—one on each side of the spillway—were also finished. In 1967, construction of a third power plant was begun. The building of the Grand Coulee Dam was an extraordinary engineering feat. Even the spillway gates—the structures that allow the water to flow over the dam—were huge.

Location: Grand Coulee, Washington
Completed: December 31, 1941
Height: 550 feet
Length: 5,223 feet
Cost: $1 billion
Fun fact: The dam is about as high as a 46-story building.

Opposite page:
The enormous spillway gates are clearly visible in this aerial photo of the Grand Coulee Dam.

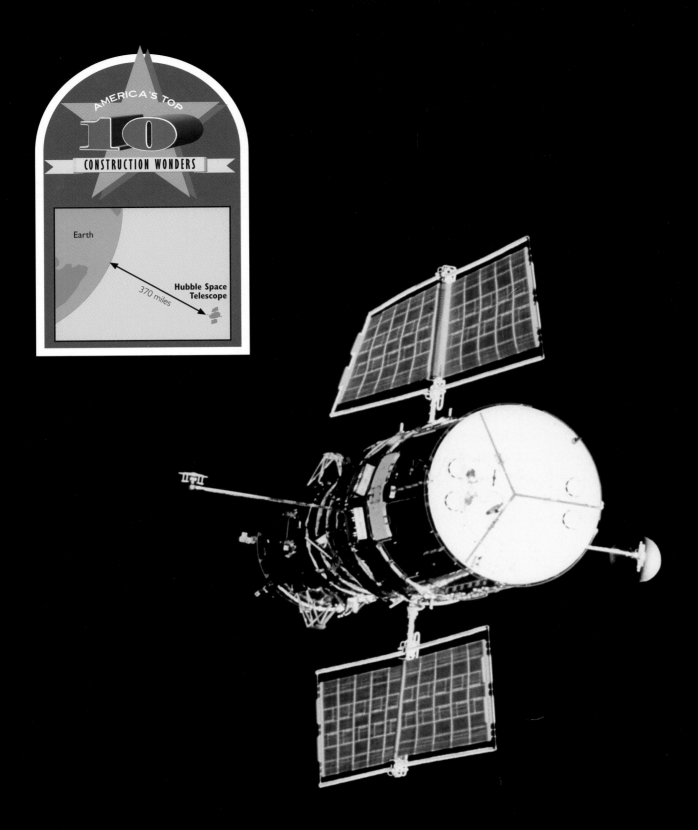

AMERICA'S TOP

10

CONSTRUCTION WONDERS

Earth

370 miles

Hubble Space Telescope

The
Hubble Space Telescope

In 1946, the astronomer Lyman Spitzer dreamed of building the first space platform that would circle the earth. It would be equipped with instruments for probing the universe. Spitzer's goal was to be able to view the skies without interference from the earth's atmosphere. The National Aeronautics and Space Administration (NASA) developed a design for the telescope, and in 1977 Congress approved the spending of federal money for the project. The telescope was named for Edwin Powell Hubble, the astronomer who found that there were galaxies beyond our own.

The Hubble Space Telescope, like many telescopes, uses mirrors to reflect light rays. The Hubble has an 8-foot primary, or main, mirror and a secondary mirror, which reflect light to various cameras and other instruments. The telescope is 4 stories tall. It is housed in an aluminum cylinder that is 14 feet wide and 43 feet long. Power is supplied by solar panels.

The Hubble was launched in April 1990. In June 1990, it began sending back its first, blurry pictures of space. This was happening because the primary mirror had been ground 10 thousandths of an inch too flat. In December 1993, the space shuttle *Endeavor* took 7 astronauts to repair the telescope. Billions of television viewers watched in amazement as they performed detailed work while floating in space. The astronauts succeeded in repairing the Hubble.

Since then, the Hubble Space Telescope has been sending remarkable images of objects in space back to Earth.

Launched: April 24, 1990
Height: 4 stories
Weight: More than 12 tons
Speed: 17,500 miles per hour
Cost: $1.5 billion
Fun fact: The "vision reach," or distance, the telescope can "see" is 12 billion miles.

Opposite page:
The Hubble Space Telescope transmits crystal-clear images of planets, galaxies, and other objects in space.

AMERICA'S TOP
10
CONSTRUCTION WONDERS

CANADA   VT ME
              NH
NY   MA
        CT
PA
    NJ   Lincoln
MD   Tunnel

The
Lincoln Tunnel

★ ★ ★ ★ ★ ★ ★ ★ ★ ★ ★ ★ ★ ★

Named for Abraham Lincoln, the Lincoln Tunnel is the longest motor vehicle tunnel in America. In April 1930, studies were done on how to ease traffic between New York City's borough of Manhattan and the state of New Jersey. The Holland Tunnel already connected these 2 points, and it was decided that another tunnel was needed to link midtown Manhattan and New Jersey.

In 1934, work began on the project. Rock was blasted away from both sides of the Hudson as workers headed toward the river bottom. Next, a pre-made steel tunnel "shield" was inserted into the floor of the Hudson River, which took out chunks of the riverbed, allowing workers to move forward underneath the water.

Once it was finished, the hole for the tunnel was lined with concrete. Steel beams were then put in to support the roadway above. This left space for a fresh-air duct under the roadway. Air was drawn in from the outside and blown into the duct. Exhaust fans removed polluted air from the tunnel. In December 1937, the first of 3 tunnel tubes was ready, but completion of the project was delayed by problems. The roadways approaching the first tube had not been finished, which slowed approaching traffic. Fewer vehicles traveled through the tunnel than expected. As a result, fewer tolls were collected and lack of money became a problem. The third tube was not built until the mid-1950s. Today, the Lincoln Tunnel handles 40 million vehicles each year, making it the busiest tunnel in the United States.

Location: Between New York City and Weehauken, New Jersey
Opened: December 22, 1937
Length: 1.5 miles
Traffic: About 40 million vehicles per year
Cost: $75 million
Fun fact: 84 giant fans replace the air in the tunnel every 90 seconds.

Opposite page:
About 40 million cars drive through the Lincoln Tunnel every year.

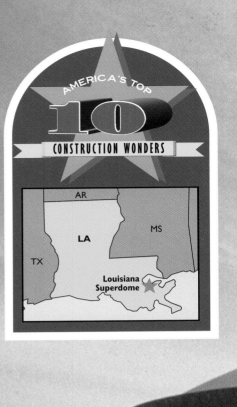

Louisiana Superdome

★ ★ ★ ★ ★ ★ ★ ★ ★ ★ ★ ★ ★ ★ ★ ★ ★ ★ ★

The Louisiana Superdome, in New Orleans, Louisiana, is the largest arena ever built. The stadium covers 13 acres and can hold up to 95,000 people.

The idea for the Superdome came from a New Orleans businessman named Dave Dixon, who wanted to bring professional football to the city. Construction began in August 1971, and the Superdome was opened 4 years later. Today, it is home to the New Orleans Saints football team. Several Super Bowl games have been held there, in addition to professional basketball, baseball, and gymnastics events.

Because New Orleans was built on what was once swampland, there were certain challenges to constructing the Superdome. For example, most stadiums have playing fields that are below street level. The Superdome's playing field, however, needed to be at street level so that it wouldn't become too damp. A complex system of columns and braces, and the domed roof, were needed to ensure the building's stability. The roof sits on a supporting structure called a tension ring. This ring rests on 96 columns arranged in a circle. The Superdome is shaped like a flying saucer. The walls hang from the roof, which is the largest steel dome in the world. The most exciting moment during construction of the arena was in 1973, when the temporary roof supports were removed. Everyone stopped working to see if the roof would be able to stand on its own! The roof held, and the Superdome was opened to the public in 1975, on August 3.

Location: New Orleans, Louisiana
Dedicated: August 3, 1975
Height: 27 stories
Diameter of dome: 680 feet
Interior space: 125 million cubic feet
Cost: $163 million
Fun fact: The dome contains 400 miles of electrical wiring.

Opposite page:
The Superdome rises 27 stories at its highest point.

AMERICA'S TOP

10

CONSTRUCTION WONDERS

WI

IA

Sears Tower

MI

OH

IL

IN

MO

KY

The Sears Tower

The Sears Tower is the tallest building in America. By the late 1960s, the Sears Company had grown so large that it needed a new building for its 13,000 employees in the Chicago area. Some of the world's best engineers and architects were hired to work on the project.

Fazlur Khan, an engineer originally from Bangladesh, made it possible for the Sears Tower to reach its impressive height of 1,454 feet. Instead of using a traditional steel skeleton, he came up with a way to connect a series of tubes that were lighter and stronger. The diagonal supports for these tubes were designed to help the building withstand strong winds. Khan's design also used "setbacks" to increase the building's stability. As the building rose, each new level was set back from the level below, which made the Sears Tower resemble a staircase. The design of the project was so far ahead of its time that engineers thought robots would be able to deliver the mail—an interesting but unworkable idea!

Construction of the Sears Tower was dangerous. Workers scaled ropes and walked on narrow beams more than 1,000 feet above the ground. As the building grew in height, it took too much time for the construction workers to climb down for lunch, so kitchens were built on both the 33rd and 66th floors. On some days, high winds stopped construction.

In 1973, on May 3—just 3 years after the project was begun—the last beam was put into place. It was signed by 12,000 construction workers, Sears employees, and Chicago's mayor.

Location: Chicago, Illinois
Dedicated: May 3, 1973
Height: 1,454 feet
Weight: More than 222,500 tons
Engineer: Fazlur Khan
Architects: Skidmore, Owings, and Merrill
Number of stories: 110
Number of visitors: 1.5 million per year
Cost: More than $150 million
Fun fact: The tower contains 25,000 miles of plumbing pipe, 2,000 miles of electric wiring, and 145,000 light fixtures.

Opposite page:
The Sears Tower reaches the highest point in Chicago's skyline.

America's Top **10** Construction Wonders

CANADA

Seattle
Space
Needle

WA

ID

OR

The Seattle Space Needle

★ ★ ★ ★ ★ ★ ★ ★ ★ ★ ★ ★ ★ ★ ★ ★

When the Seattle Space Needle was built for the 1962 World's Fair in Seattle, it was the tallest building west of the Mississippi River. The theme for the fair was science and technology. At the time, the Soviet launch of the first human-made satellite, *Sputnik*, had spurred the United States to join the "space race." Organizers of the fair thought that a space-aged structure would thus be a good centerpiece for the fair.

The first phase of construction involved excavation. At the end of 11 days, a 30-foot-deep hole covered the entire site. In order to stabilize the tall and slender Space Needle, the underground foundation had to weigh as much as the above-ground structure. To accomplish this, 250 tons of steel reinforcing bars and 72 anchor bolts were set into the hole before the concrete was poured. Then, in May, about 5,850 tons of concrete were poured for 12 straight hours.

Each of the steel beams made for the Space Needle was 90 feet long and weighed 27,000 pounds! To form the upper sections, which curve outward, the straight beams were heated and then bent. Once all the construction problems were solved, the Space Needle rose quickly. By September, it was 200 feet tall. The restaurant and observation decks, located more than 500 feet up from the ground, were completed in December. The last piece of steel added was the 50-foot torch tower. The Space Needle was the hit of the World's Fair. Almost 20,000 people rode its elevators every day to the observation level!

Location: Seattle, Washington
Dedicated: April 21, 1962
Height: 605 feet
Designer/Architects: John Ridley and Victor Steinbrueck
Number of visitors: 1.4 million visitors per year
Cost: About $4.5 million
Fun fact: It took 3,700 tons of steel to build the Space Needle.

Opposite page:
Today, the Space Needle is the symbol of Seattle.

America's Top 10 Construction Wonders are not necessarily the largest, but at the time they were built, they were extraordinary engineering feats. Below is a list of 10 other notable construction projects.

More American Construction Wonders		
Name	**Location**	**Description**
Cathedral of St. John the Divine	New York City	When finished, it will be the largest cathedral in the world.
Golden Gate Bridge	San Francisco, California	Second-longest bridge in America at 4,600 feet.
Hoover Dam	Colorado, Arizona, Nevada	Second-highest dam in America at 726 feet.
Houston Astrodome	Houston, Texas	First domed sports stadium.
Mount Washington Cog Railway	White Mountains, New Hampshire	The first cog railway in America rises 3,625 feet.
Oroville Dam	Feather, California	Highest dam in America at 770 feet.
Rockefeller Center	New York City	Occupies more than 22 acres and has 19 buildings.
Verrazano-Narrows Bridge	New York City	Longest bridge in America at 4,260 feet.
Washington Monument	Washington, D.C.	Tallest stone structure in the world at 555 feet.
World Trade Center	New York City	Second-tallest building in America at 1,377 feet.

See page 229 for more information about construction wonders.

AMERICA'S TOP

10

CURIOSITIES

AMERICA'S TOP

10

CURIOSITIES

NM		OK		AR
	TX			
	Austin's		LA	
	Bat Colony ★			
MEXICO			Gulf of Mexico	

Austin's Bat Colony

One of nature's most spectacular sights can be seen in downtown Austin, Texas, on a summer evening. Around sunset, thousands of bats emerge from cracks beneath the Congress Avenue Bridge, which spans Town Lake. Forming as many as 5 long columns, the bats fly off into the night.

Austin's colony is the largest urban bat colony in the world. Up to 1.5 million Mexican free-tail bats live underneath the bridge. The adults weigh about half an ounce and have average wingspans of 12 inches.

The bats arrive in mid-March, after leaving their winter homes in Mexico. In early summer, the females give birth to babies, called "pups." When the pups are 5 weeks old, they learn how to fly and how to navigate using reflected sound— a process called "echolocation." By August, the pups are ready to hunt for food with their mothers. This is the best time to see large groups of bats flying away from the bridge. By early November, as the weather cools, the bats leave Austin and fly to Mexico for the winter.

Bats first began living beneath the Congress Avenue Bridge many years ago. The colony grew rapidly after the bridge was rebuilt in 1980. Some people were frightened when they saw so many bats and wanted the bat colony destroyed. They changed their minds, however, when they learned that Mexican free-tail bats are gentle animals and seldom harm people. In fact, Austin's bats are very helpful. Every night they eat up to 30,000 pounds of mosquitoes and other insects!

Name: Often called "the Congress Avenue Bridge bat colony"

Location: Texas

Size of colony: 250,000 to 1.5 million, depending on the time of year

When the bats are seen: From mid-March to early November. The best time is early evening, especially during July and August.

Fun fact: Mexican free-tail bats travel as far as 800 miles between their summer and winter homes.

Opposite page: City residents gather to witness the dramatic flight of the bats at sunset.

OR
ID
WY
SD
NE
NV
UT
CO
CA
AZ
NM
Pacific
Ocean
MEXICO
TX

Bristlecone Pines

★ ★ ★ ★ ★ ★ ★ ★ ★ ★ ★ ★ ★ ★ ★ ★ ★

Bristlecone pines are the oldest trees in the world. Some are 5,000 years old—and still growing! They are found at high altitudes on dry mountains in the American Southwest. Bristlecone pines grow very slowly. One 700-year-old tree studied by scientists was only 3 feet tall and its trunk was only 3 inches wide. To find out the age of a living tree, scientists first drill out a cylinder, or core, of wood. The core is then examined under a microscope to determine the number of annual rings.

There are 2 species, or kinds, of bristlecone pines. The Rocky Mountain bristlecone grows in Colorado and Utah. The Great Basin bristlecone is found mainly in the White and Panamint Mountains of southeastern California. The oldest bristlecone pines are found in the White Mountains. These trees have strange, twisted shapes, and they are dead except for a narrow core of living bark. This bark carries water from the soil up through the trunk. These pines may have just one living branch and only a few twigs that bear needles. The dead wood of a bristlecone pine does not rot easily, however, but remains solid, and supports the tree's living parts.

Young bristlecone pines have green, smooth bark. As the trees age, their bark becomes scaly. Although most pine trees keep their needles for 2 or 3 years, bristlecone pine needles remain on the trees for 12 to 20 years. When they are about 20 years old, these trees begin producing hard, reddish-brown cones. These cones have sharp, bristle-like prickles, for which the trees are named.

Name: For the bristle-like prickles on the pine cones.
Location: American Southwest (California, Arizona, New Mexico, Nevada, Colorado, Utah)
Age: Up to 5,000 years
Height: Usually less than 50 feet
Cones: 1.5 to 3.5 inches long
Fun fact: A bristlecone pine that is no taller than a human may be more than 900 years old.

Opposite page:
The ancient bristlecone pines in the White Mountains are the oldest trees on earth.

AMERICA'S TOP
10
CURIOSITIES

MT
ND
MN
WY
SD
Flaming
Fountain
NE
IA

The Flaming Fountain

★ ★ ★ ★ ★ ★ ★ ★ ★ ★ ★ ★ ★ ★ ★ ★

On the grounds of the state capitol in Pierre, South Dakota, is America's most curious fountain. This fountain is created by water that flows from an underground source. The water is burning hot and contains natural gas.

Hot underground water is common in the prairies of South Dakota. Early pioneers discovered that this water could be used for heating. In the early 1900s, engineers drilled a well next to the capitol. The water was used to heat the capitol and other buildings. This method didn't work, however, because chemicals in the water corroded the pipes and other equipment.

In the 1950s, after an explosion occurred in one of the buildings, the heating system was abandoned. Now the hot water runs underground and into Capitol Lake. The water contains so much natural gas that it can be ignited at the point where it comes out of the ground. Once lit, it burns continuously. Today the Flaming Fountain is the center of a memorial honoring veterans of the Korean and Vietnam Wars.

The one problem with the Flaming Fountain is that it smells terrible! The water that bubbles out of the ground contains so much sulfur that people standing near the fountain sometimes get headaches or become nauseated from the fumes. Fortunately, the fumes cannot be smelled from the edge of Capitol Lake. Because most of the lake water comes from the fountain, ice doesn't form unless the temperature falls below 10 degrees Fahrenheit. The area near the fountain never freezes.

Name: Recognizes the ability of the sulfurous water to burn

Location: South Dakota

Temperature of water coming from the ground: 100 to 112 degrees Fahrenheit

Created: In the early 1900s

Fun fact: Natural gas is a fossil fuel. It is formed from the remains of organisms that lived millions of years ago.

Opposite page:
The flaming fountain burns because its water source contains natural gas.

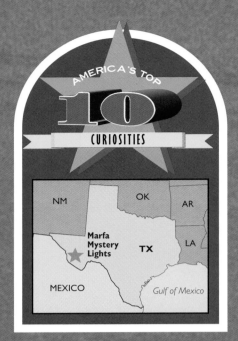

America's Top 10 Curiosities

Marfa Mystery Lights

NM   OK   AR
        TX
            LA
MEXICO   Gulf of Mexico

Marfa Mystery Lights

On many evenings, and in all kinds of weather, strange lights can be seen near the base of the Chianti Mountains in western Texas. They appear soon after sunset and continue until dawn. The lights seem to be suspended in the air. They glow brightly, bounce around, flicker, disappear, and then suddenly reappear. Accounts of the lights vary widely. They have been described as white lights and colored lights, as single lights and clusters of lights. Some people say that the lights look like small balls of fire while others say they are as big as basketballs. The lights have been said to glow softly and to dance like candle flames.

The lights are always viewed from the same site—about 10 miles east of the small town of Marfa. No one, however, can identify the source or location of the lights. In fact, the lights disappear or move out of reach whenever they are approached.

No one knows how long the mystery lights have been appearing. The Apaches saw them in the 1800s and maybe even earlier. In 1883, a man named Robert Ellison reported seeing the lights, and since then, thousands of people have also viewed them. The lights have even become a popular tourist attraction.

Although no one knows why the lights appear, many explanations have been proposed. The Apaches believed the lights to be falling stars. Others have suggested that lightning or other atmospheric phenomena are the cause. Stranger explanations include glow-in-the-dark rabbits, the ghosts of dead lovers, and visitors from outer space.

Name: Honors Marfa, a town about 10 miles west of the lights
Location: Texas
When the lights are seen: Between sunset and midnight
Discovered: Probably in the early 1800s
Fun fact: The town of Marfa was named by an engineer's wife for the heroine in a Russian novel.

Opposite page:
These lights, which have been witnessed for hundreds of years, have never been explained.

AMERICA'S TOP
10
CURIOSITIES

NV | UT | CO
CA
**Meteor
Crater** ★
AZ | NM
MEXICO

★ ★

Meteor Crater

About 50,000 years ago, an object from outerspace crashed into the earth, blasting a hole in the middle of the Arizona desert. Scientists call this hole the Barringer Meteorite Crater after the engineer who first proposed that it was produced by a meteorite. (Any object that travels through the earth's atmosphere and hits the ground is called a meteorite.) Most people simply call the hole Meteor Crater.

The meteorite that created the crater was an asteroid—a small, planet-like object that orbits the sun. Because asteroids travel very fast, they do not have to be large to cause a lot of damage. The asteroid that created Meteor Crater is believed to have been about 150 feet in diameter and traveling at approximately 40,000 miles per hour when it hit the ground. The collision destroyed most of the asteroid, leaving only small fragments. These tiny pieces show that the object from space was made mostly of iron and nickel.

The crater looks like a giant bowl. It is 560 feet deep and 4,180 feet across. Its rim rises 160 feet above the surrounding plain. This hole is big enough to hold 20 football fields, and could seat 2 million people on its sloping sides!

Meteor Crater played a role in America's Apollo Space Program, which sent men to the moon. Apollo astronauts were trained in Meteor Crater to learn about the geology of craters caused by asteroids.

Name: Honors mining engineer Daniel Moreau Barringer
Location: Arizona
Depth: 560 feet
Width: 4,180 feet
Discovered: Originally by Native Americans (date unknown); first written report in 1871
Fun fact: Meteor Crater is deep enough to contain the Washington Monument.

Opposite page:
Meteor Crater is Earth's largest, best-preserved crater made by an asteroid.

AMERICA'S TOP

10

CURIOSITIES

OR
ID
CA
NV
UT
Mystery
Spot
Pacific Ocean
AZ
MEXICO

The Mystery Spot

The force of gravity pulls objects toward the center of the earth. Because of gravity, people stand perpendicular to the ground and not at an angle. Gravity also causes balls to roll downhill rather than uphill. At the Mystery Spot, near Santa Cruz, California, however, objects roll uphill and people appear to lean backwards or sideways. Even the trees do not grow perpendicular to the ground!

Have the laws of gravity gone haywire at the Mystery Spot? Different theories have been proposed to explain the phenomenon there, but so far none have been proven. The most widely believed explanation is that there are magnetic rocks beneath the ground—perhaps remains of a meteorite—that interfere with the force of gravity and cause it to pull at an unusual angle.

Walking through the Mystery Spot is an eerie experience. People must lean to maintain their balance, and when walking uphill, they must climb straight-legged.

One popular demonstration at the Mystery Spot shows the strange forces at work there. Two bricks are placed on the ground and are shown to be level with each other. When 2 people of equal height stand on the bricks, 1 person appears to be taller. When they switch places, however, the person who appeared taller now looks several inches shorter!

Even airplanes flying overhead are affected by the strange forces at the Mystery Spot. Their compasses sometimes swing as much as 40 degrees off course!

Name: Recognizes that the cause of this curiosity is still a mystery
Location: California
Size of area: About 150 feet in diameter
Discovered: 1940
Fun fact: Some people say they get headaches or upset stomachs in the Mystery Spot. Other people say they feel better there than they do anywhere else!

Opposite page:
An official guide at the Mystery Spot shows one of the strange effects there. The guide is not intentionally leaning, nor does he fall over.

AMERICA'S TOP

10

CURIOSITIES

CANADA

ME

VT

★

**Old Man
of the
Mountain**

NH

*Atlantic
Ocean*

NY

MA

The Old Man of the Mountain

The official symbol of the state of New Hampshire is the 40-foot-high rock face of the Old Man of the Mountain. It is formed from 6 huge granite slabs that jut out from a cliff in the shape of a man's profile. The Old Man of the Mountain was first discovered by the Abenaki tribe. Later, in 1805, Francis Whitcomb and Luke Brooks noticed the profile while working on a road through Franconia Notch—a narrow pass in the White Mountains. They thought it looked like Thomas Jefferson, who was president of the United States at the time.

The Old Man of the Mountain was carved by nature. About 50,000 years ago, a large glacier, or sheet of ice, moved through Franconia Notch. It removed huge amounts of soil and rock from the mountain, leaving behind the rough outlines of a face. The finer details were carved by a combination of freezing and thawing.

To help protect the Old Man's profile, some of the rocks have been braced with cables and anchor irons. Cracks are sealed with a tough substance called epoxy. Aqueducts made of stone and cement have been built on top of the mountain to direct water away from the face.

The Old Man of the Mountain is best viewed from the shore of Profile Lake. This lake is 1,200 feet below the Old Man, at the base of Cannon Mountain. Millions of people have come here to see and photograph the granite profile. Many have read Nathaniel Hawthorne's story, called *The Great Stone Face*, which was inspired by this natural curiosity.

Name: Based on a story by Nathaniel Hawthorne
Location: New Hampshire
Height of face: 40 feet
Discovered: Originally, by the Abenaki tribe (date unknown); later 2 surveyors, Francis Whitcomb and Luke Brooks, in 1805.
Fun fact: Cannon Mountain is named for a horizontal rock that juts out from the mountainside and looks like the barrel of a cannon.

Opposite page:
The striking granite features of the Old Man were carved entirely by natural forces.

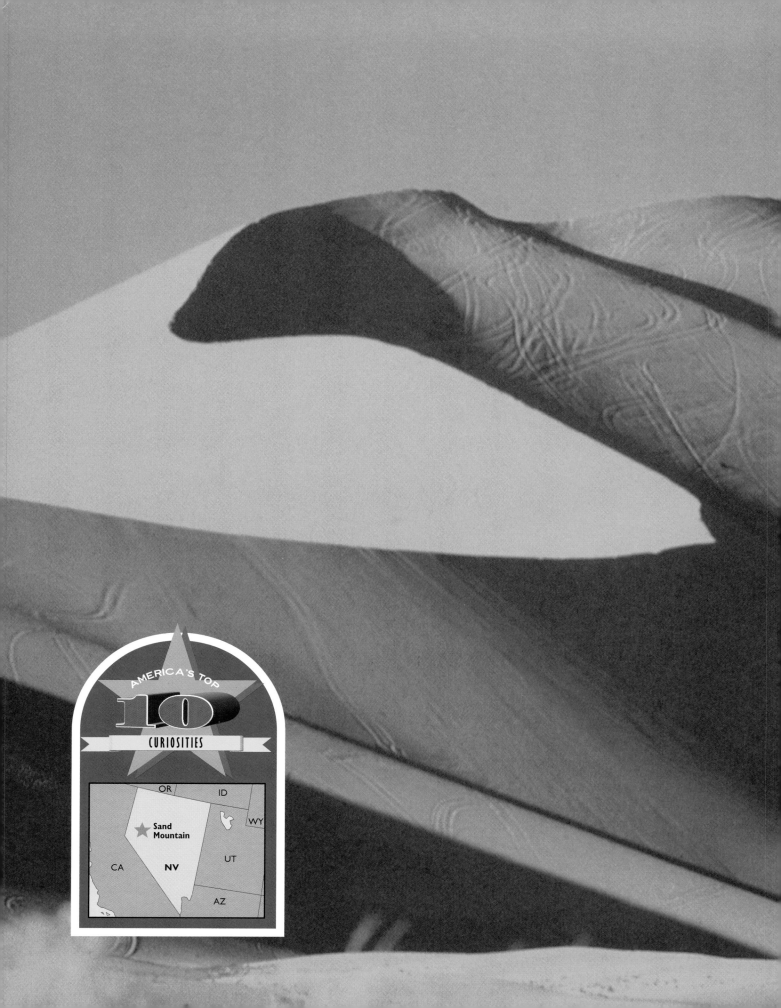

AMERICA'S TOP

10

CURIOSITIES

Sand
Mountain

OR   ID

WY

UT

CA   NV

AZ

Sand Mountain

The stretch of U.S. Highway 50 that crosses Nevada is known as "the loneliest highway in America." It passes dry sagebrush, deserted mining towns, and a hill that makes strange noises. This hill, called Sand Mountain, is in western Nevada, about 25 miles southeast of the town of Fallon. The "mountain," known as "seif" dune for its long, sword-like shape, is actually a sand dune about 600 feet high and 2.5 miles long.

Walk up Sand Mountain, and you'll hear all kinds of noises that sound like moans, booms, and loud roars. These sounds come from beneath your feet. Some of them are so loud that they can be heard up to 7 miles away!

The sounds occur when the sand moves—for example, when people walk over it, animals run across it, or wind pushes it around. The rubbing together of the sand particles produces the sounds.

The musical sands of Sand Mountain are a natural curiosity, but they are not unique. There are musical sands in other parts of the world. Scientists have discovered two kinds of musical sands. Dry and highly polished sand particles—such as those that make up Sand Mountain—produce low, booming sounds. Particles that are large and almost perfectly round produce high, squeaky sounds.

No one knows when Sand Mountain was first discovered. It was probably known to Native Americans who lived in the area centuries ago. Early pioneers who travelled through the area probably heard the musical sounds, along with riders on the Pony Express.

Name: Known as "seif" dune, after the Arabic word "sayf," meaning sword.
Location: Nevada
Size: About 600 feet high and 2.5 miles long
Discovered: Date unknown. The first written description was in 1883.
Fun fact: One of the residents of Sand Mountain is the Sand Mountain blue butterfly, which feeds on buckwheat.

Opposite page:
Some of the strange sounds made on Sand Mountain can be heard up to 7 miles away.

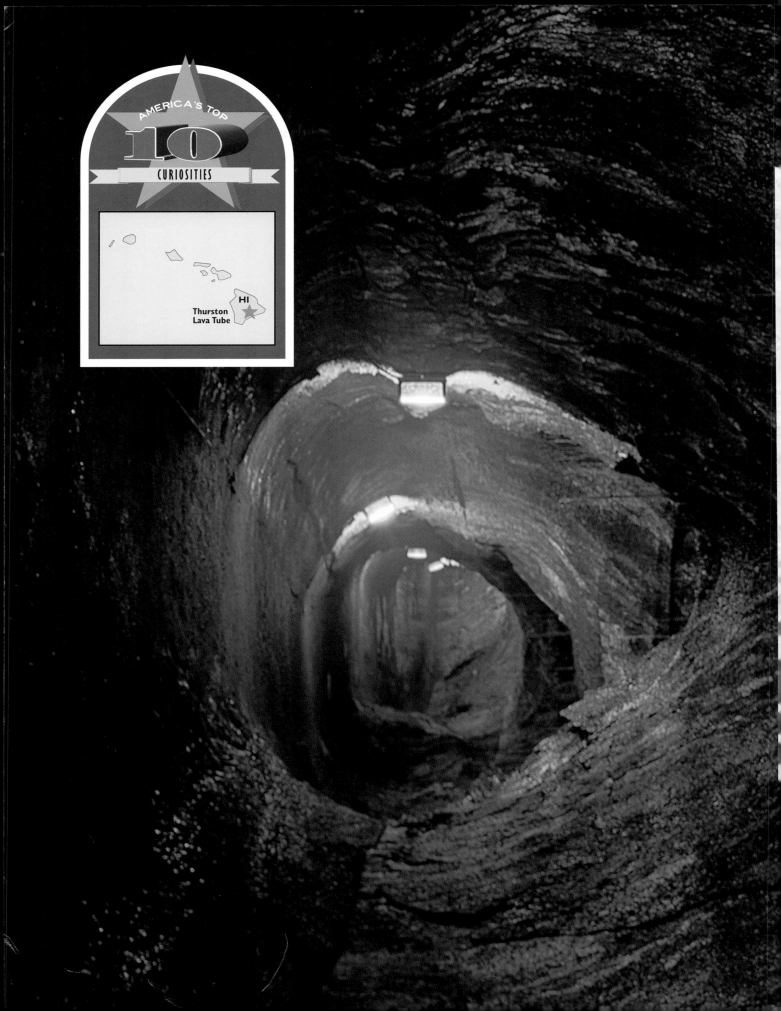

AMERICA'S TOP

10

CURIOSITIES

HI

Thurston
Lava Tube

Thurston Lava Tube

★ ★ ★ ★ ★ ★ ★ ★ ★ ★ ★ ★ ★ ★ ★ ★ ★ ★ ★

On Hawaii's Big Island lies an ancient tunnel. It's about 450 feet long—about 90 feet longer than a football field—with a ceiling at least 10 feet high. In some places, the tunnel is as wide as a living room. This tunnel is the Thurston Lava Tube, also known by its Hawaiian name, Nahuku. It was formed during an eruption of the volcano Kilavea that created the Big Island.

Far below the earth's crust are areas of hot, molten (liquid) rock. This molten rock comes to the surface through cracks in the crust. At the surface, it is called "lava." Sometimes lava shoots out in violent eruptions. The Hawaiian Islands were formed mainly by a series of quiet eruptions. The lava poured out from openings in the tops and sides of the volcanoes and flowed downhill toward the sea. This process is still taking place on the Big Island today.

Lava from the Big Island's erupting volcanoes flows in two ways: It either spreads out in puddles or runs in streams through narrow channels. Lava tubes are formed by several processes. Sometimes the lava on the surface of a lava stream cools and hardens, while the lava below the hardened surface remains molten and continues to flow—just as water flows through a pipe. When the eruption ends, or the lava finds another path, the molten lava drains out, leaving a hardened tunnel, or lava tube.

Close examination of the interior of the Thurston Lava Tube shows how it was shaped by various flows. The marks on the walls indicate how the lava stream eroded the ground.

Name: Honors publisher Lorrin A. Thurston, who began an effort to make the lava tube and its surroundings a public park. Nahuku, its Hawaiian name, means "the protuberances."
Location: Hawaii
Length: About 450 feet
Height: 6–12 feet
Fun fact: Lava tubes usually are widest and deepest near the vent of a volcano. They become narrower and more shallow farther away.

Opposite page:
Lava tubes can be as large as a whole house.

AMERICA'S TOP
10
CURIOSITIES

MT

★ Yellowstone
Lake Whispers

ID

SD

WY

NE

UT

CO

Yellowstone Lake Whispers

Can a lake talk? Long ago, Native Americans heard whispering sounds near the Yellowstone and Shoshone Lakes in Wyoming. They believed that spirits were talking near the lakes. In the 1800s, fur trappers also heard the lakes "talking." In 1872, a man named F. Bradley described the phenomenon as "a hoarse whine." Then in 1893, Edwin Linton wrote about "a strange echoing sound in the sky." Other people have compared the sounds to bells, harps, humming bees, and rushing wind.

No one knows what produces the sounds. The most likely cause might be wind blowing across the lakes or over the surrounding mountains. But there is no evidence of wind when the sounds are heard. Leaves on the trees do not move, nor are ripples seen on the lakes.

Another theory suggests that the sounds originate far below the earth's surface, where there is molten, or hot liquid, rock. This liquid rock heats water under the ground in the Yellowstone region that eventually comes to the surface in the form of hot springs, such as geysers. Heat escapes from the water when it reaches the earth's surface, and this may produce the whispering sounds. These sounds are heard only near the two lakes, however, and never near the geysers.

Because the sounds are soft and usually do not last longer than half a minute, they are difficult to hear. They are most often heard early in the morning in a quiet area. The sounds are rarely heard in the summer, when the park is filled with tourists.

Name: Describes the soft sounds heard near Yellowstone Lake and Shoshone Lake
Location: Wyoming
Discovered: By Native Americans (date unknown)
Fun fact: In the middle of winter, when Yellowstone Lake is covered with thick ice, some spots on the lake bottom are near boiling point.

Opposite page:
No one knows what produces the whispering sounds around the Yellowstone and Shoshone lake region.

The 10 curiosities in this book are all naturally occurring phenomena. They were chosen for a number of different reasons, such as uniqueness, age, size, geological interest, and mysterious quality. Below is a list of more curiosities.

More American Curiosities

Name, Location, *Description*

Alaskan Peninsula, Alaska. *Longest peninsula.*

Bagley Icefields, Alaska. *Largest icefield.*

Big Room at Carlsbad, New Mexico. *Largest cave room.*

Cape Disappointment, Washington. *Foggiest place.*

Columbia Glacier, Alaska. *Fastest moving glacier.*

Crater Lake, Oregon. *Deepest lake.*

Death Valley, California. *Lowest spot.*

El Capitan, California. *Largest block of granite.*

Everglades, Florida. *Largest marsh.*

Grand Canyon, Arizona. *Largest gorge.*

Great Salt Lake, Utah. *Largest inland body of salt water.*

Lachuguilla Cave, New Mexico. *Deepest cave.*

Lake Michigan, Illinois, Indiana, Michigan, Wisconsin. *Largest lake.*

Landscape Arch, Utah. *Longest natural arch.*

Lost Sea, Tennessee. *Largest underground lake.*

Mammoth Cave National Park, Kentucky. *Most extensive cave system.*

Mauna Loa, Hawaii. *Largest active volcano.*

Mississippi River, Minnesota, Wisconsin, Iowa, Illinois, Missouri, Kentucky, Tennessee, Arkansas, Mississippi, Louisiana. *Longest river.*

Mississippi River delta, Louisiana. *Largest delta.*

Mojave Desert, California. *Largest desert.*

Molokai sea cliffs, Hawaii. *Highest sea cliffs.*

Mount McKinley, Alaska. *Highest mountain.*

Mount Waialeale, Hawaii. *Wettest place.*

New River, West Virginia. *Deepest river.*

North Fork Roe River, Montana. *Shortest named river.*

Ribbon Falls, California. *Highest continuous waterfall.*

Sea Lion Cave, Oregon. *Largest sea cave.*

Steamboat Geyser, Wyoming. *Tallest active geyser.*

Yellowstone, Montana, Wyoming. *Largest geothermal basin.*

Landscape Arch

See page 230 for more information about curiosities.

AMERICA'S TOP

10

MOUNTAINS

AMERICA'S TOP

10

MOUNTAINS

ID

★ Grand
Teton

MT

WY

SD

NE

UT

CO

Grand Teton

★ ★ ★ ★ ★ ★ ★ ★ ★ ★ ★ ★ ★ ★ ★ ★ ★ ★

Magnificent Grand Teton towers over Wyoming's Teton Range and the surrounding countryside. Its jagged peak and sheer walls can be seen 100 miles away. The most stunning views of this mountain are from the eastern base of the range.

The Tetons began forming about 9 million years ago, which makes them some of the youngest mountains in America. They are called "fault-block" mountains because they were pushed up from the earth's crust by a series of earthquakes. The fault line lies along the eastern base of the range, and this side of the mountain rises sharply. Grand Teton's eastern slope rises about 7,000 feet from the valley below.

At an elevation of 13,770 feet above sea level, Grand Teton is separated from its neighbor, Middle Teton, by a pass called Lower Saddle. At 13,200 feet, not far from Grand Teton's summit, a smaller pass called Upper Saddle separates the mountain's main peak from a smaller peak to the west. Just above Upper Saddle is a narrow ledge named the Crawl. Many adventurous people who climb Grand Teton wriggle along this ledge on their stomachs!

Grand Teton's main peak is rough and almost pointed. It is a very windy spot. Although a lot of snow falls on the peak, most of the snow is blown away by the wind.

At lower altitudes, Grand Teton is covered by forests. Pines, firs, and aspen are the dominant trees. Tree line—the point above which it is too cold for trees—is at 10,000 feet.

Name: From French words meaning "large breast"

Height: 13,770 feet above sea level

Location: Wyoming

Mountain range: The Teton Range, part of the American section of the Rocky Mountains

Park: Grand Teton National Park

Earliest recorded climb to the summit: By William O. Owen and 3 other men in 1898

Wildlife: Bald eagle, bighorn sheep, elk, marmot, moose, mule deer, pronghorn antelope

Fun fact: Native Americans called the Teton Range Teewinot, which means "many pinnacles."

Opposite page:
Grand Teton is the highest peak in the Teton Range.

AMERICA'S TOP

10

MOUNTAINS

MO

TN

Magazine
Mountain

OK

AR

MS

TX

LA

Magazine Mountain

★ ★ ★ ★ ★ ★ ★ ★ ★ ★ ★ ★ ★ ★ ★ ★ ★ ★

Most of the central United States consists of vast, grassy plains of flat or gently rolling land. But in the south-central part of the country are the Ozark Mountains. They stretch across northern Arkansas and southern Missouri and include parts of Oklahoma and Kansas. The tallest of the Ozarks is Magazine Mountain. Although this is the highest point between the Appalachian Mountains, to the east, and the Rocky Mountains, to the west, Magazine Mountain rises only 2,753 feet above sea level. In a sense, the Ozarks aren't really mountains. They were formed from a plateau that rose up from the surrounding land—geologists say this land was "uplifted." Rivers eroded some areas of the plateau more than others, creating valleys and "mountains."

Magazine Mountain sits between two river valleys: the Arkansas River valley to the north, and the Petit Jean River valley to the south. A scenic road crosses the mountain from north to south. The top of Magazine Mountain is mostly flat. Travelers can park their cars there, and then take a short walk up to Signal Hill, the mountain's peak.

The mountain is covered by forest. Pine, oak, and hickory are the most common trees. The oak and hickory trees on the mountaintop are much smaller than those on the slopes, even though many are as old—or older. The trees are stunted because the mountaintop's climate is harsh. Dogwood trees also grow on Magazine Mountain, and in spring they are covered with blossoms.

Name: Believed to be named for its resemblance to a magazine—a fort-like building where goods are stored

Height: 2,753 feet above sea level

Location: Arkansas

Mountain range: Boston Mountains, part of the Ozarks

Park: Ozark National Forest

Average annual snowfall: Several inches

Wildlife: Armadillo, barred owl, black bear, great horned owl, opossum, raccoon, red-tailed hawk, squirrel, white-tailed deer

Fun fact: The Diana butterfly and a small snail called the Magazine Mountain shagreen can be found only on Magazine Mountain.

Opposite page:
Many of the trees on Magazine Mountain turn golden in the fall.

AMERICA'S TOP

10

MOUNTAINS

Mauna
Kea

HI

Mauna Kea

★ ★

High above the town of Hilo, on the island of Hawaii, is Mauna Kea. This volcano rises 13,796 feet above sea level. It is the highest mountain in the world if it is measured from its base on the ocean floor, rather than at sea level. Mauna Kea began forming when hot liquid rock, called lava, poured out of cracks on the Pacific Ocean floor. Gradually, over hundreds of thousands of years, the lava accumulated, and the mountain grew. It broke through the surface of the water and kept rising. From its base, Mauna Kea measures 33,500 feet high!

The road leading to the top of Mauna Kea passes through many different environments. On the mountain's lower slopes are sugar-cane fields and grasslands. Further up the slope, more lava is visible. It comes in many colors—black, brown, red, and silver—and in many shapes. Plants have broken down the older lava, creating soil. Ferns and ohia bushes covered with red blossoms decorate the landscape. Closer to the summit, there are no plants. Some of the wildlife on Mauna Kea are found nowhere else in the world. One, a bird called the palila, lives at least 6,000 feet above sea level.

At 13,020 feet lies Lake Waiau—the third-highest lake in the United States. The summit of Mauna Kea provides spectacular views across the island of Hawaii toward the Pacific Ocean. The air on the summit is very clear, and many telescopes have been placed there. The Mauna Kea Observatory Complex includes two Keck telescopes—the largest telescopes ever built.

Name: From Hawaiian words meaning "white mountain"
Height: 13,796 feet above sea level
Location: Hawaii
Mountain range: None
Parks: Pohakuloa State Park, State Science Reserve Area
Wildlife: Hawaiian goose, mouflon sheep, pheasant, wild pig
Fun fact: In 1996, an astronomer using the Mauna Kea Observatory discovered the first brown dwarf, an object in outer space that is bigger than a planet but not quite a star.

Opposite page:
Mauna Kea can be seen clearly from the lava-covered base of Mauna Loa, which is another volcano.

AMERICA'S TOP

10

MOUNTAINS

WY

NE

UT

CO

★ Mount
Elbert

KS

AZ

NM

OK

Mount Elbert

★ ★

Mount Elbert, located in central Colorado, is the highest peak in the American part of the Rocky Mountains, which also extend north into Canada. It is a fairly easy mountain to climb. Three trails lead to the summit, which is 14,433 feet above sea level.

The summit of Mount Elbert is large and broad. Its height makes weather harsh—it is usually very windy on top of the mountain. Below, patches of snow sometimes remain on the ground even in warm weather. Every so often, snow falls in the middle of summer!

Mount Elbert is part of the Sawatch Mountains, the tallest of the many ranges that make up the Rockies. This range runs along the Continental Divide—the "backbone of America." All the rivers on the west side of this imaginary line flow toward the Pacific Ocean. Those on the east side flow toward the Gulf of Mexico and the Atlantic Ocean. Mount Elbert is just to the east of the Continental Divide. The streams that originate on the mountain, such as Elbert Creek and Bartlett Gulch, eventually empty into the Arkansas River. This river—one of America's longest—flows into the Mississippi, which empties into the Gulf of Mexico.

The lower elevations of Mount Elbert are covered by forest. Lodgepole pine, Engelmann spruce, and aspen are the most common trees there. The tree line is at an elevation of between 11,000 and 12,000 feet. Above that, large areas are filled with alpine wildflowers.

Name: Honors Samuel H. Elbert, a public official in Colorado during the 19th century.
Height: 14,433 feet above sea level
Location: Colorado
Mountain range: Sawatch Mountains (part of the American Rockies)
Park: San Isabel National Forest
Wildlife: Badger, deer, eagle, elk, fox, goshawk, porcupine, ptarmigan, weasel
Fun fact: The Sawatch range includes 15 mountains that are 14,000 feet or more in height, which is a record for the United States.

Opposite page:
Nestled in the American Rockies, Mount Elbert creates a high point.

AMERICA'S TOP

10

MOUNTAINS

AK

CANADA

Mount
McKinley

Mount McKinley

laska's Mount McKinley (known in Alaska as Denali) is America's highest mountain. South Peak, the taller of its twin peaks, soars 20,320 feet above sea level. Two miles away is North Peak, which is somewhat lower. Separating the peaks is Denali Pass.

Mount McKinley is part of the Alaska Range. These mountains are called "uplift mountains." They began forming about 60 million years ago when two plates, or pieces, of the earth's crust collided. This forced huge masses of rock upward. About 2 million years ago, new plate collisions started, which are still occurring, thrusting the Alaska Range even higher.

Since the Alaska Range first began taking shape, the mountains have been eroded by running water, such as streams. Mount McKinley is composed mainly of granite—a hard rock that erodes more slowly than other kinds of rock. For this reason, the mountain stands more than 3 miles above the surrounding land.

Mount McKinley is so high that on clear days it can be seen more than 100 miles away. Most of the time, however, it is hidden from view by fog and clouds. Severe storms in the area, sometimes lasting for weeks, are common.

Snow and ice cover Mount McKinley year-round. No one knows exactly how much snow falls on the summit, however, because weather equipment cannot function in the high winds at the top. At the base of the mountain, which is 7,200 feet above sea level, as much as 8 feet of snow may fall in a single snowstorm.

Name: Honors William McKinley, 25th president of the United States
Height: 20,320 feet above sea level
Location: Alaska
Mountain range: Alaska Range
Park: Denali National Park
Earliest recorded climb to the summit: By Hudson Stuck, Walter Harper, Harry Karstens, and Robert Tatum in 1913
Wildlife: Bald eagle, black bear, finch, raven
Fun fact: Aleuts—natives of Alaska—named this mountain Denali, "the high one."

Opposite page:
A clear view of Mount McKinley's peak is a rare sight.

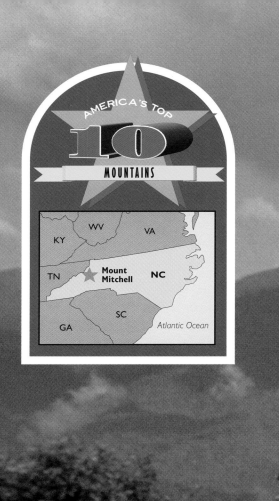

America's Top

10

MOUNTAINS

Mount Mitchell

KY · WV · VA · TN · NC · SC · GA · Atlantic Ocean

Mount Mitchell

★ ★ ★ ★ ★ ★ ★ ★ ★ ★ ★ ★ ★ ★ ★ ★ ★

Mount Mitchell is the tallest mountain east of the Mississippi River. It is located in the Black Mountains of western North Carolina. These mountains are named after the dark green forests that cover their summits, making the mountains appear black.

The Black Mountains are the highest section of the Blue Ridge Mountains, which are famous for their beauty. In spring and early summer, mountain laurel, azalea, and masses of rhododendron are in bloom. The Blue Ridge is part of the Appalachians, a chain of mountain ranges that is about 1,500 miles long. It runs parallel to the Atlantic Ocean, from Canada to Alabama.

The Appalachians are called "folded mountains." They were formed when pressure under the earth's surface pushed the rock layers upward, causing them to fold over. Long ago, the Appalachians were much higher than they are today. For millions of years, they have been worn down (eroded) by glacial action and running water.

On the summit of Mount Mitchell is a gray stone tower. It was built in memory of Elisha Mitchell, for whom the mountain is named. When the sky is clear, there are spectacular views from the summit, although the mountain is often blanketed by clouds and fog.

Red spruce and Fraser fir are the most common trees in the dense forests of Mount Mitchell. Many of these trees are covered with small organisms called "lichens," which come in many shapes. Some cling like barnacles to tree trunks. Others hang from branches in thread-like masses.

Name: Honors Elisha Mitchell, who measured the mountain's height in 1835
Height: 6,684 feet above sea level
Location: North Carolina
Mountain range: Black Mountains—part of the Blue Ridge Mountains, in the Appalachian mountain range
Parks: Mount Mitchell State Park and Pisgah National Forest
Average annual snowfall: About 104 inches
Wildlife: Black bear, bobcat, deer, grouse, raven, squirrel, white-tailed deer
Fun fact: During the Ice Age that ended about 11,000 years ago, saber-toothed tigers and mastodons roamed the Black Mountains.

Opposite page:
Like other mountains in the Appalachian range, Mount Mitchell has been eroded by glaciers.

AMERICA'S TOP
10
MOUNTAINS

CANADA

★ Mount
Rainier   **WA**

OR   ID

Mount Rainier

★ ★ ★ ★ ★ ★ ★ ★ ★ ★ ★ ★ ★ ★ ★ ★ ★

Mount Rainier is one of America's most beautiful mountains. Located near Seattle, Washington, it is the highest mountain in the Cascade Range. When the sky is clear, Mount Rainier's snow-covered peak can be seen for hundreds of miles in all directions.

The mountain is actually a volcano that started forming about 1 million years ago. It grew larger and larger as layer after layer of molten rock spouted from an opening in the earth's crust. Mount Rainier's last major eruptions occurred about 2,000 years ago, but smaller ones took place within the past 200 years. Today, steam rises from the 2 craters on the summit, which suggests that the volcano may erupt again.

The upper slopes of Mount Rainier are covered with snow and ice year-round. The summit is broad and rounded and has 3 peaks. Columbia Crest is the highest. The other 2 are Liberty Cap and Point Success.

Many glaciers have formed on the mountain. The longest is Carbon Glacier. The largest is Emmons Glacier. One of the fastest moving is Nisqually Glacier. As the glaciers move, they erode the underlying rock, changing the shape of the mountain. In warm weather, huge masses of ice and snow break off from glaciers and tumble down the mountainside. On the lower slopes of Mount Rainier are meadows filled with colorful wildflowers in spring and summer. Below the tree line—at about 6,000 feet—are forests of tall evergreens. The forests and surrounding foothills are often covered by fog.

Name: Given by British navigator George Vancouver in honor of his friend, British Rear Admiral Peter Rainier

Height: 14,410 feet above sea level

Location: Washington

Mountain range: Cascade Range

Park: Mount Rainier National Park

Average annual snowfall: More than 45 feet

Earliest recorded climb to the summit: By Hazard Stevens and Philemon Beecher Van Trump in 1870

Wildlife: Chipmunk, horned lark, marmot, mountain goat, pika, ptarmigan, rosy finch, squirrel, water pipit

Fun fact: Native Americans called this mountain Tahoma, which means "the mountain that was God."

Opposite page:
Mount Rainier stands on a flat plateau, separated from other peaks in the Cascade Range.

AMERICA'S TOP
10
MOUNTAINS

AK   Mount
        Saint
        Elias   CANADA

Mount Saint Elias

The second-highest peak in the United States is Mount Saint Elias, which lies on the border between Alaska and Canada, near the Gulf of Alaska. Emptying into the gulf is Icy Bay, named for the many icebergs that float in its waters. These giant chunks of ice break off, or calve, from glaciers on Mount Saint Elias and other mountains in the Saint Elias range. When a chunk of ice calves and falls into the water, it makes a thunderous splash.

The largest glacier in the region is the vast Malaspina Glacier, along the southern base of the mountain. This glacier is larger than the state of Rhode Island! Smaller glaciers that are moving down the sides of Saint Elias and neighboring mountains feed into Malaspina Glacier.

The Saint Elias Mountains are called "uplift mountains" because they formed when two plates of the earth's crust collided. Masses of rock were forced upward, creating the mountains.

Mount Saint Elias is comparatively young. It has steep cliffs and jagged peaks that have not yet been worn down by erosion. Most of Mount Saint Elias is covered with snow year-round. This surface snow often hides deep crevasses, or narrow openings, which can be death traps for careless climbers. Another danger is avalanches—masses of snow, ice, and other materials that tumble swiftly down a mountainside. The Saint Elias Mountains have some of the worst weather in the world. Huge storms sweep in from the Pacific Ocean, bringing violent winds and heavy snowfall.

Name: Honors a Catholic saint
Height: 18,008 feet above sea level
Location: Alaska
Mountain range: Saint Elias Mountains
Park: Wrangell—Saint Elias National Park
Earliest recorded climb to the summit: By a group led by Prince Luigi Amedeo of Savoy, Duke of the Abruzzi, in 1897
Wildlife: Caribou, Dall sheep, eagle, hawk, Steller jay, wolf
Fun fact: Wrangell—Saint Elias National Park is America's largest national park. It is more than 3 times as big as Yellowstone National Park.

Opposite page:
The snow-covered peak of the mountain rises into the clouds.

AMERICA'S TOP

10

MOUNTAINS

CANADA

ME

VT

Mount
Washington

NY

NH

*Atlantic
Ocean*

MA

Mount Washington

At 6,288 feet above sea level, Mount Washington is the highest mountain in New England. It is part of the northern Appalachians.

Mount Washington is an old mountain that was formed more than 350 million years ago. When it was young, it was much higher than it is today. Over hundreds of millions of years, however, the mountain has been worn down by erosion. Many of its features were created by the movement of glaciers that once covered its slopes. These large "rivers" of ice carved several enormous, bowl-shaped valleys called "cirques" into the sides of the mountain. The last glaciers melted about 12,000 years ago.

Forests cover Mount Washington's slopes to an elevation of about 3,300 feet above sea level. Above the tree line is tundra, where only mosses, grasses, and other low-growing plants can survive. The layer of soil on the tundra is thin, and the summer growing season is short. In spite of these harsh conditions, many small, beautiful flowering plants are found among the rocks.

The summit of Mount Washington is famous for its howling winds. In winter, they often blow at a speed of 200 miles per hour. In summer, it is fairly easy to climb to the top, where there is a weather station and an observation center. One of the most interesting ways to reach the summit is on the Mount Washington Cog Railway, which has been operating since 1869. It takes the railway 3 hours to climb to the top of the mountain and then return to the base.

Name: Honors George Washington, first president of the United States

Height: 6,288 feet above sea level

Location: New Hampshire

Mountain range: Presidential Range in the White Mountains, which are part of the Appalachians

Park: Most of the mountain is in White Mountain National Forest.

Average annual snowfall: 255 inches

Earliest recorded climb to the summit: By Darby Field and 2 others in 1642

Wildlife: Beaver, black bear, crow, deer, fox, hawk, moose, raccoon, raven

Fun fact: The first passenger vehicle reached the summit in 1861. It was a stagecoach drawn by 8 horses.

Opposite page:
The sugar maple trees on the lower slopes of Mount Washington turn red in the fall.

AMERICA'S TOP

10

MOUNTAINS

OR
ID
CA
NV
UT
Mount
Whitney
Pacific Ocean
AZ
MEXICO

Mount Whitney

★ ★ ★ ★ ★ ★ ★ ★ ★ ★ ★ ★ ★ ★ ★ ★ ★ ★

America's tallest mountain outside Alaska is Mount Whitney. It is part of a great mountain range called the Sierra Nevada, Spanish for "snowy, saw-toothed mountain range." The Sierra Nevada range is located along the eastern border of California. The mountains in this range are called "fault-block mountains" because they formed along a fault, or crack, in the earth's crust. Millions of years ago, earthquakes along the fault line lifted and tilted a block of rock hundreds of miles long that became the Sierra Nevada. The mountain slopes facing the fault—the eastern side of the range—rise almost straight up. The eastern side of Mount Whitney rises abruptly from Owens Valley for about 11,000 feet. The western side slopes much more gradually.

Mount Whitney is in the southern part of the Sierra Nevada, near Death Valley. It is not particularly distinctive when viewed from afar. Up close, however, Mount Whitney is very dramatic, because it rises so abruptly. Its beauty may explain why it is the most frequently climbed mountain in the Sierra Nevada.

The lower slopes of the mountain are covered with evergreen forests. Only small plants survive above the tree line, at about 11,000 feet. Even at the summit, however—14,494 feet above sea level—flowering plants have taken root. The summit is nearly flat and is covered with several acres of large rocks. An average of 150 to 200 inches of snow fall there each year. Although the mountain is not covered with snow year-round, it has several glaciers and permanent snowfields.

Name: Honors Josiah D. Whitney, who helped found the California Geological Survey in 1860

Height: 14,494 feet above sea level

Location: California

Mountain range: Sierra Nevada

Park: Sequoia and Kings Canyon National Park

Earliest recorded climb to the summit: By Charles D. Begole, Albert H. Johnson, and John Lucas in 1873

Wildlife: Deer, marmot, pica, rosy finch, squirrel, vole

Fun fact: Begole, Johnson, and Lucas climbed Mount Whitney because they wanted to escape the hot weather at lower elevations.

Opposite page:
Mount Whitney is the tallest American mountain outside Alaska.

AMERICA'S TOP

10

NATIONAL MONUMENTS

OR   ID

NV   UT

CA

Pacific Ocean

Cabrillo
National
Monument

AZ

MEXICO

The Cabrillo National Monument

More than a million people visit the Cabrillo National Monument each year. Many of them come to catch a glimpse of the 2,000 gray whales that migrate past this location along the California coast between December and February. There is also an unusual tidal pool at this site, with a unique and rich variety of animal and plant species.

The Cabrillo National Monument was established in 1913 on Point Loma, at the entrance to present-day San Diego Bay. Point Loma was first discovered by the Portuguese explorer Juan Rodriguez Cabrillo, who anchored his ship near the spot. He was the first explorer to travel to the west coast of what is now the United States and is credited with discovering California in 1542, on September 28.

By the 1850s, there were so many boats traveling in this area that a lighthouse was built on Point Loma, 422 feet above the sea. It operated until 1891, when a new lighthouse was built on lower land so its light could shine under the fog. The original lighthouse is a favorite spot for visitors.

At the monument's visitors center there is a popular museum where visitors can watch a movie that tells the story of Juan Rodriguez Cabrillo. There is also a scenic overlook and a 14-foot-high statue of the Portuguese explorer. The statue is a replica of one created by the sculptor Alvaro DeBree in 1939. (The original statue was severely worn by the weather.) Each September, during the Cabrillo Festival, a re-enactment of Cabrillo's arrival at Point Loma is performed.

Location: San Diego, California
Size: 144 acres
Number of visitors: More than 1 million per year
Established: 1913
Height of statue: 14 feet
Weight of statue: 7 tons
Sculptor: Alvaro DeBree
Fun fact: Between 21,000 and 25,000 gray whales migrate through the eastern Pacific Ocean. About 10 percent are seen at the monument.

Opposite page:
The lighthouse on Point Loma is a popular stop for tourists.

AMERICA'S TOP

10

NATIONAL MONUMENTS

NE   IA
          IL
      MO
KS   George
      Washington
      Carver National
OK   Monument
      AR   TN   KY

The George Washington Carver National Monument

The George Washington Carver National Monument is the first national monument for an African American. It was created in 1943 to honor an African-American scientist who made many contributions to the field of agriculture. The monument is located at George Washington Carver's birthplace in Diamond, Missouri.

Carver was born a slave in the early 1860s and was raised by the Carver family, who owned him. After the Civil War, Carver left Diamond to study botany (the science of plants). In 1896, he went to Alabama to teach at the Tuskegee Institute. While at Tuskegee, Carver studied farming so that he could teach African Americans to become successful farmers and raise crops other than cotton. He discovered 325 new uses for peanuts and 118 ways to use sweet potatoes!

The idea for a monument to honor Carver came from a man named Richard Pilant. In the early 1940s, Pilant wrote over 700 letters to members of Congress urging them to establish a monument in Carver's honor. His efforts were successful and the George Washington Carver Memorial Associates was formed soon after.

The monument consists of 210 acres that were once part of the original Carver farm, where the scientist was born and lived as a child. On this land is a statue of Carver as a boy, the birthplace cabin site, an 1881 historic house, and the Carver family cemetery. Visitors to the George Washington Carver National Monument can walk along trails that lead them past all these sights.

Location: Diamond, Missouri
Size: 210 acres
Number of visitors: About 50,000 per year
Dedicated: July 14, 1953
Height of statue: 5 feet
Sculptor: Robert Amendola
Fun fact: One of the products Carver made from peanuts was instant "coffee."

Opposite page:
The statue of George Washington Carver as a boy sits on the land where Carver spent his childhood.

AMERICA'S TOP

10

NATIONAL MONUMENTS

MD

D.C.

Jefferson
Memorial

VA

The Jefferson Memorial

★ ★ ★ ★ ★ ★ ★ ★ ★ ★ ★ ★

Thomas Jefferson was the nation's third president and the main author of the Declaration of Independence. He was also one of Colonial America's strongest supporters of freedom and equality. This monument to him was started in 1938 and was dedicated 5 years later, on April 13, 1943—the 200th anniversary of Jefferson's birth. The white marble building, with its 26 columns and dome, is similar in style to Monticello, Jefferson's Virginia home. (Look at the back of a nickel to see what Monticello looks like.) Located on a bank of the Tidal Basin in Washington, D.C., the monument is especially beautiful when it is lighted at night.

Above the entrance to the memorial, is a sculpture that shows Jefferson standing with Benjamin Franklin, John Adams, Robert Livingston, and Roger Sherman. These men helped to write the Declaration of Independence. Engraved on 4 marble panels on the inner walls are quotations from the Declaration and other writings of Jefferson's. (There are 11 mistakes on these panels. If you visit, see if you can find them.) A 5-ton, 19-foot bronze statue of Jefferson stands in the memorial's center.

According to the memorial's original plans, the beautiful Japanese cherry trees that lined the Tidal Basin were to be torn down. Protestors chained themselves to these trees, and as a result, most of the trees were left standing. Each year, thousands of people visit Washington, D.C., just to see the trees in full bloom during the Cherry Blossom Festival.

Location: Washington, D.C.
Number of visitors: About 600,000 per year
Dedicated: April 13, 1943
Materials: White marble, black granite, and bronze
Height of statue: 19 feet
Weight of statue: 5 tons
Sculptor: Rudulph Evans
Cost: $3.2 million
Fun fact: The memorial was designed by John Russell Pope, Otto R. Eggers, and Daniel P. Higgins.

Opposite page:
The Jefferson Memorial was designed to look like Jefferson's home in Virginia.

AMERICA'S TOP

10

NATIONAL MONUMENTS

MD

D.C.

Lincoln
Memorial

VA

IN THIS TEMPLE
AS IN THE HEARTS OF THE PEOPLE
FOR WHOM HE SAVED THE UNION
THE MEMORY OF ABRAHAM LINCOLN
IS ENSHRINED FOREVER

The Lincoln Memorial

The Lincoln Memorial is the most-visited tourist site in Washington, D.C. It was built in honor of America's 16th president, Abraham Lincoln, who guided the country through the Civil War. Since its dedication in 1922, this memorial has been a symbol of freedom. In 1963, on August 28, Martin Luther King, Jr.—a leader of the civil rights movement—gave his famous "I Have a Dream" speech at the memorial to a crowd of more than 200,000 people.

The memorial stands at the west end of the Reflecting Pool, which runs all the way to the Washington Monument. In 1867, 2 years after Lincoln was killed, Congress started making plans for the memorial's construction. The design was not completed until 1912, however, and work did not begin until 1914.

The marble building was designed to look like the Parthenon Temple in Greece. It has 36 exterior columns, which represent the 36 states in the Union at the time of Lincoln's death. Its 56 stone steps symbolize Lincoln's age when he died. In the monument's inner room is a white marble statue of Lincoln. The president's second inaugural speech and his Gettysburg Address are engraved on the walls there.

Underneath the Lincoln Memorial is a cave that contains beautiful limestone formations called stalagmites and stalactites. The stalagmites grow up from the floor, and the stalactites hang from the ceiling. These incredible cave formations developed from water dripping into the storage area underneath the structure.

Location: Washington, D.C.
Number of visitors:
    About 6 million per year
Dedicated: May 30, 1922
Material: White marble
Height of statue: 19 feet
Weight of statue:
    900 tons
Sculptor: Daniel Chester French
Cost: Almost $3 million
Fun fact: The Lincoln Memorial is sited so that it is directly in line with the nation's Capitol and with the Washington Monument.

Opposite page:
A large, white marble statue of Lincoln looks out from the memorial's inner room.

AMERICA'S TOP

10

NATIONAL MONUMENTS

WY

NE

UT

CO

KS

Mesa Verde
National Park

AZ

NM

OK

Mesa Verde National Park

Mesa Verde National Park is a monument to the Anasazi Indians. Sometimes called the "ancient ones," the Anasazi lived in what is now Colorado nearly 2,000 years ago. The park sits on a plateau and is home to the best-preserved cliff dwellings in the United States. The plateau was named Mesa Verde, or "green table," by Spanish explorers in the 18th century. All together, more than 4,000 prehistoric sites are preserved in the park.

The Anasazi began to settle in the caves at Mesa Verde in about A.D. 1. As time passed, they built complex structures from adobe clay and stone. Entire towns were built right into the cliffs. Many cliff houses are connected, creating "apartment buildings" several stories high. At the bases of these structures, the Anasazi built kivas, which are ceremonial chambers. Cliff Palace is the most amazing of the Anasazi dwellings. It has more than 200 rooms, 23 kivas, many storage chambers, and open-air courtyards. Scientists have not been able to discover why, but around A.D. 1300, the Anasazi abandoned their cliff homes. They resettled in what are now New Mexico and Arizona.

Mesa Verde National Park preserves all the cliff dwellings at this 52,000-acre site. Visitors can also see pottery and other artifacts made by the Anasazi. In 1978, Mesa Verde was named a World Heritage Cultural Site by the United Nations. Every year in July, there is a 3-day Indian Arts and Crafts Festival at the park.

Location: Southwestern Colorado
Size: 52,000 acres
Number of visitors: About 600,000 per year
Established: 1906
Fun fact: The black-and-white pottery produced by the Anasazi are among the finest ancient pots made in North America.

Opposite page:
Cliff Palace is a spectacular example of the ancient cliff houses built by the Anasazi Indians.

AMERICA'S TOP

10

NATIONAL MONUMENTS

MT
ND
MN
WY
SD
★ Mount
Rushmore
NE
IA

Mount Rushmore

★ ★ ★ ★ ★ ★ ★ ★ ★ ★ ★ ★ ★ ★ ★ ★

Mount Rushmore National Memorial, in the Black Hills of South Dakota, honors 4 of America's most popular presidents. Carved in the granite mountain cliff are the faces of George Washington, Thomas Jefferson, Abraham Lincoln, and Theodore Roosevelt. Doane Robinson had the idea for the monument in 1924. He chose Gutzon Borglum to be the sculptor, and Borglum decided whose portraits would be carved.

The first face sculpted out of the cliff was George Washington's. Jefferson's was done next, to the left of Washington's, but the sculptor had difficulty with the rock. Jefferson's entire head had to be blasted away! It was then carved to the right of Washington. Lincoln's portrait was chiseled next, followed by Roosevelt's.

During the project, workers were strapped into special chairs (called bosun chairs). With safety lines, they were then lowered down the mountain. Suspended in this way, they drilled, hammered, and chiseled the stone.

It took almost 400 workers 6½ years of actual working time to finish the project, but because of money problems, it was 14 years before the memorial was completed. In 1941, on March 6, Borglum died at the age of 74. His son Lincoln continued in his father's place, and Mount Rushmore was finished that October.

In 1991, on July 3, a formal dedication was held in honor of the memorial's 50th anniversary. Nineteen of the men who built the memorial attended the celebration.

Location: The Black Hills of South Dakota
Number of visitors: Almost 3 million per year
Dedicated: August 10, 1927
Completed: October 31, 1941
Material: Granite
Height of carvings: 60 feet
Height of mountain: 5,725 feet
Sculptor: Gutzon Borglum
Cost: About $1 million
Fun fact: More than 450,000 tons of rock were removed from the mountain.

Opposite page:
The faces of 4 of America's most popular presidents are carved into the Black Hills of South Dakota.

The Statue of Liberty

★ ★ ★ ★ ★ ★ ★ ★ ★ ★ ★ ★ ★

The Statue of Liberty is one of the most famous landmarks in the world. In 1864, a Frenchman named Edouard-René Lefebvre de Laboulaye wanted to find a way to honor the friendship between France and America that began during the American Revolution. The sculptor Frédéric-Auguste Bartholdi came up with the idea for the statue and completed its first model by 1870.

Bartholdi decided to place the statue on an island in New York harbor. It had once been used by Native Americans and was called Oyster Island. The French planned to fund the statue, and the Americans agreed to pay for its pedestal.

Bartholdi built the statue in sections. The arm and the torch were ready by 1876. They were sent to Philadelphia for America's centennial (100th birthday) celebration. The statue was completed in France in August 1884.

The fundraising process for the pedestal did not go smoothly in America. In 1885, the well-known publisher, Joseph Pulitzer, promised to print in his newspaper the names of everyone who contributed to the project. In just 5 months, more than $100,000 was raised from the donations of 120,000 people.

In 1885, on June 17, the statue, packaged in separate sections, arrived in New York harbor. Once the pedestal was finished in 1886, assembly of the statue began. It took 75 workers 6 months to complete the job. One hundred years later, in 1986, a rededication ceremony was held on Liberty Island to celebrate this symbol of American freedom and independence.

Location: Liberty Island, New York harbor
Number of visitors: 3 million per year
Dedicated: October 28, 1886
Materials: Copper, iron
Height of statue alone: 151 feet
Height including pedestal: 305 feet
Weight of statue: 225 tons
Weight of pedestal: 27,000 tons
Number of steps: 154
Sculptor: Frédéric-Auguste Bartholdi
Cost: $650,000
Fun fact: There are 354 steps from the lobby to the crown of the statue.

Opposite page:
The Statue of Liberty stands as a welcome to travelers entering New York harbor.

The Vietnam Veterans Memorial

In Washington, D.C.'s Constitution Gardens, between Constitution Avenue and the Reflecting Pool, is the Vietnam Veterans Memorial. Many people feel that this monument is the most touching memorial in Washington, D.C. The monument is black granite and is shaped in a V. The 58,156 names of all the men and women who are missing from, or who lost their lives in, the Vietnam War are inscribed on the monument wall. These names are listed in the order in which these Americans were lost.

The monument originally consisted of the granite wall and a life-size bronze statue by Frederick Hart of 3 soldiers—1 white, 1 African American, and 1 Hispanic. In 1993, a sculpture by Glenna Goodacre was added, honoring the estimated 10,000 women who served.

Jan Scruggs, a Vietnam War veteran, had the idea for the new monument. A contest was held for its design, which was won by Maya Ying Lin, a 21-year-old student at Yale University. The memorial was dedicated on Veterans Day in 1982. During the 5-day ceremony, all of the names inscribed on the wall were read aloud—which took 60 hours.

The lettering on the memorial is small because Lin wanted people to get close to the wall in order to read the names. She thought this would help them to have a quieter, more personal experience. Thousands of people visit this memorial each year. Relatives and friends of people inscribed on the wall often leave flowers and letters in memory of their loved ones.

Location: The Mall, Washington, D.C.
Number of visitors: About 1.2 million per year
Dedicated: Veterans Day 1982
Material: Black granite
Shape: The letter V
Length: 492 feet
Number of names inscribed: 58,156
Number of panels: 140
Designer: Maya Ying Lin
Cost: About $7 million
Fun fact: Maya Ying Lin received only a B- from an art professor for the design of this celebrated memorial.

Opposite page:
A total of 58,156 names are listed on the Vietnam Veterans Memorial.

AMERICA'S TOP
10
NATIONAL MONUMENTS

MD

D.C.

VA

Washington
Monument

The Washington Monument

★ ★ ★ ★ ★ ★ ★ ★ ★ ★ ★ ★ ★ ★

The Washington Monument, at just over 555 feet tall, is the tallest masonry (stone) structure in the world. It is also one of the world's most popular tourist attractions. The marble walls at its base are 15 feet thick and 55 feet wide. Each of the 50 flags flying along the base represents one of the states in the Union.

The huge monument was built to honor our nation's first president. Although it was originally planned in 1783, it took more than 100 years to complete. In 1833, the Washington National Monument Society was created to raise money for the project. Individual donations were limited to $1 so that every American could participate. When enough money was raised to begin, a design contest was held. It was won by an architect named Robert Mills. A time capsule was built into the cornerstone (the first stone laid in a foundation). Among the contents of the capsule were copies of the Declaration of Independence and the U.S. Constitution.

In the 1870s, after the Civil War, enough money was raised to continue construction of the monument. In 1884, on August 9, the last stone was set at a height of 500 feet. Four months later, on December 6, the pyramid section was secured on top and the Washington Monument was completed. It was dedicated on Washington's Birthday—February 21, 1885—and was opened to the public by 1888.

Today, the monument is one of the most popular attractions in Washington, D.C. On average, 25 people visit it every 5 minutes!

Location: Washington, D.C.
Number of visitors: More than 1 million per year
Dedicated: February 21, 1885
Material: Marble
Height: 555 feet, 5 inches
Weight: 90,854 tons
Shape: Obelisk
Number of steps: 898
Designer: Robert Mills
Cost: Almost $1.2 million
Fun fact: The ceremony marking the completion of the Washington Monument was held in gale-force winds.

Opposite page:
The Washington Monument is an obelisk, a design first used by the Ancient Egyptians.

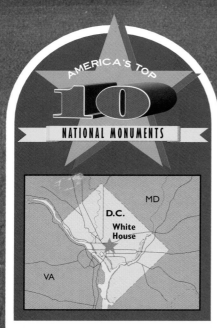

AMERICA'S TOP
10
NATIONAL MONUMENTS

MD

D.C.
White House

VA

The White House

★ ★ ★ ★ ★ ★ ★ ★ ★ ★ ★ ★ ★ ★

The White House is one of the most important symbols of our nation. Its history dates back to 1791, when Washington, D.C., was chosen as the site for the nation's capital. In that same year, a design contest was held, which James Hoban won. The house was ready for its first occupants in 1800—the family of John Adams, the second president.

During the War of 1812, British troops set fire to the president's house. James Madison's wife, Dolley, managed to save several historic paintings before the house burned to the ground. In 1815, construction of a new house began at the same site. It was finished 5 years later. This new white building was nicknamed "The White House." In 1902, that became its official name.

There have been many important and interesting "firsts" in the White House. Our seventh president, Andrew Jackson, was the first to have indoor running water. In 1818, during President Rutherford B. Hayes's term, the first telephone was installed. In 1891, Benjamin Harrison, our 23rd president, was the first to have electric lighting installed.

In 1948, Harry Truman and his family moved out of the White House while it was being rebuilt. After 4 years of renovation, the building looked much as it does today. Since then, several First Ladies have decorated it, beginning with Jacqueline Kennedy, who founded the White House Historical Association in 1961. Among the 132 rooms are the Oval Office—where the president works— a bowling alley, movie theater, and game room.

Location: 1600 Pennsylvania Avenue, Washington, D.C.
Number of visitors: As many as 10,000 per day; about 1.5 million per year
Number of employees: About 345,000
Number of rooms: 132
Original Designer: James Hoban
Fun fact: About 50,000 calls per day are received at the White House.

Opposite page:
The White House is considered to be a symbol of the American presidency.

America's Top 10 Monuments are not necessarily the 10 "best." They pay tribute to people who have made important contributions to the nation's history and culture. Below is a list of other notable monuments and memorials.

More American Monuments & Memorials		
Name	**Location**	**Description**
Aztec Ruins National Monument	New Mexico	Preserves the ruins of the Anasazi, including a multistory pueblo with about 400 rooms.
Booker T. Washington National Monument	Virginia	The birthplace and boyhood home of the great African-American educator.
Clara Barton National Historic Site	Maryland	The home of the founder of the American Red Cross.
Confederate Monument	Georgia	Life-size statues of Civil War generals Robert E. Lee, Stonewall Jackson, Thomas R.R. Cobb, and W.H.T. Walker.
Devils Tower National Monument	Wyoming	The core of an ancient volcano.
Effigy Mounds National Monument	Iowa	191 prehistoric Native American burial mounds.
Eleanor Roosevelt National Historic Site	New York	Eleanor Roosevelt's home.
Fort Sumter National Monument	South Carolina	The first shots of the Civil War were fired here on April 12, 1861.
Korean War Veterans Memorial	Washington, D.C.	A tribute to the people who served in the Korean War.
Martin Luther King, Jr. National Historic Site	Georgia	The civil rights movement leader's birth place, church, and gravesite.
USS Arizona Memorial	Hawaii	Honors those who died in the attack on Pearl Harbor during World War II.
Wright Brothers National Memorial	North Carolina	The site at Kitty Hawk, where Orville and Wilbur Wright flew the first airplane.

Confederate Monument

Wright Brothers National Memorial

See page 231 for more information about national monuments.

AMERICA'S TOP

10

NATIONAL PARKS

AMERICA'S TOP

10

NATIONAL PARKS

CANADA

ME

★ Acadia
National
Park

VT

NH

NY

Atlantic Ocean

★ ★

Acadia

The highest point on the East Coast of the United States is located atop Cadillac Mountain in Acadia National Park. For most of the year, this is the first place in the nation to be touched by the morning sun. From the summit, there are wonderful views of the surrounding forests and Acadia's dramatic coastline.

When the surf crashes against the rocky coast, it sends spray high into the air. On sunny days, the ocean sparkles. Often, however, thick fog hides the ocean from view. Even then, the waves can be heard pounding the shore. One of the noisiest places in the park is known as Thunder Hole. There, waves press against air in a cave to produce what sound like explosions. Along the shore, tidal pools can be found among the rocks. These pools are filled by ocean water twice a day during high tide. Each is a "micro-environment," containing a large variety of living things, such as tiny fish, snails, and barnacles.

Acadia has 3 main parts. One, Schoodic Peninsula, is on the mainland. Another is Mount Desert Island, which is connected to the mainland by a bridge. The third part is Isle au Haut, an island that can be reached by boat.

Inland, Acadia is covered mainly by dense forests. There are streams running through these forests. The park also has many lakes and ponds where beaver build underwater lodges.

One of the best ways to explore Acadia is to walk or bicycle along its 45 miles of carriage roads. Native plants, such as sweet fern and blueberry bushes, grow alongside these stone roads.

Name: Refers to the 17th-century French colony that included this land as well as parts of eastern Canada
Location: Maine
Established: 1919, as Lafayette National Park. Its name was changed to Acadia in 1929.
Size: About 40,000 acres
Highest point: 1,530 feet above sea level (Cadillac Mountain)
Trails: 120 miles
Number of visitors: 2.5 million per year
Rank: 8th most visited
Animals: Beaver, cormorant, coyote, deer, fox, peregrine falcon, seagull
Plants: Blueberry, fir and spruce trees, wild roses
Fun fact: There are about 300 species of birds in the park.

Opposite page:
Waves crash against
Acadia's rocky shoreline.

AMERICA'S TOP

10

NATIONAL PARKS

NV   UT   CO

CA   ★
      Grand Canyon
      National Park

      AZ   NM

MEXICO

Grand Canyon

★ ★ ★ ★ ★ ★ ★ ★ ★ ★ ★ ★ ★ ★ ★ ★

Grand Canyon National Park is home to one of the world's largest and most spectacular canyons. It is 277 miles long, more than 1 mile deep, and as much as 18 miles wide in places. This natural wonder was created millions of years ago by the Colorado River, which runs along the canyon floor. As it flowed over the land, the river cut into the rock, exposing the various layers. The rocks near the canyon ridge are about 250 million years old, while those at the bottom are almost 2 billion years old.

The landscape has undergone many changes during this 2-billion-year period. Once, there were mountains there. At other times, the land was flat and covered by water. These changes can be read in the rocks and the fossils (the remains of living things) found in the canyon walls.

The plants and animals living in the park also have stories to tell. The Kaibab squirrel and the Abert squirrel, for example, which live on opposite sides of the canyon, once had a common ancestor. As the canyon was being formed, the squirrels on the North Rim became separated from those on the South Rim. Gradually, they evolved into 2 different species. Today, Kaibab squirrels have white tails, while Abert squirrels have gray tails and white bellies.

Many visitors view the canyon only from the rim, or edge. Others go down to the floor, either on foot or riding on mules. Some people even venture down the Colorado River in a wooden boat or rubber raft.

Name: Refers to the large ("grand") canyon that is the highlight of the park
Location: Arizona
Established: 1919
Size: 1.2 million acres
Highest point along rim: 8,803 feet above sea level (Point Imperial)
Trails: About 400 miles
Number of visitors: 4.6 million per year
Rank: 2nd most visited
Animals: Coyote, mule deer, raven, squirrel
Plants: Aspen, blue spruce, and Douglas fir trees (North Rim); pinyon pine, ponderosa pine (South Rim); various cactuses (canyon floor)
Fun fact: A trip through the canyon by river raft can take 2 weeks or longer.

Opposite page:
The rock layers of the Grand Canyon glow in the light of the setting sun.

AMERICA'S TOP

10

NATIONAL PARKS

MT

★ Grand Teton
National Park

ID

SD

WY

NE

UT

CO

★ ★ ★ ★ ★ ★ ★ ★ ★ ★ ★ ★ ★ ★ ★ ★ ★ ★ ★

Grand Teton

Grand Teton National Park is named for the dramatic mountains on its western side. The Teton Range, which is part of the Rockies, is sometimes called "the American Alps." Native Americans called the range *Teewinot*, meaning "many pinnacles," because these mountains have high, jagged peaks. Many are capped with snow year-round. On still mornings, the mountains are reflected in the lakes at their bases, such as Jackson Lake.

On the eastern side is a valley through which the Snake River runs. This valley contains many different natural environments. Colorful meadows filled with sagebrush and wildflowers exist alongside cool, dark forests of pine and spruce trees. These forests are plentiful on the lower mountain slopes. At higher altitudes, only small, low-lying plants are found. It is too cold and windy on the peaks for trees and most other plants to survive.

Beavers, minks, and otters can be seen around the park's lakes and rivers. Moose, bison, and coyotes are also plentiful, as are many kinds of birds. One of the world's largest elk herds lives in the valley and in the surrounding hills. In summer, they live in the high country but return to the lowlands for the winter.

Park trails lead in all directions. Some trails run along the lakes at the mountain bases. Other trails cut into deep canyons, where colorful wildflowers grow near steep walls. Skyline Trail climbs into the highlands, where visitors find superb views of a glacier, many peaks, and Jackson Hole.

Name: Honors the highest mountain in the park
Location: Wyoming
Established: 1929
Size: 310,521 acres
Highest point: 13,770 feet above sea level (Grand Teton)
Trails: About 250 miles
Number of visitors: 3.8 million per year
Rank: 5th most visited
Animals: Bald eagle, beaver, bison, black bear, deer, duck, elk, heron, moose, pronghorn sheep
Plants: Fir and lodgepole pine trees, sagebrush plants, hundreds of wildflowers
Fun fact: The Teton Range, the youngest mountains in the Rockies, displays some of the oldest rocks in North America.

Opposite page:
The snow-capped Grand Teton Range rises dramatically from the western side of this beautiful park.

AMERICA'S TOP

10

NATIONAL PARKS

Great Smoky NC
Mountains
National Park

Great Smoky Mountains

★ ★ ★ ★ ★ ★ ★ ★ ★ ★ ★ ★ ★ ★ ★ ★

Each year, more than 9 million people visit Great Smoky Mountains National Park. It is the most frequently visited national park in the United States. The park lies in the rugged Appalachians, which is the largest mountain range in eastern United States. The Appalachian Trail runs along the top of the range, from Maine to Georgia. The trail's highest point is on the summit of Clingmans Dome, the highest mountain in the Smokies.

The Smokies are among the oldest mountains on earth. About 200 million years ago, they were much higher than they are now. Over the years, their peaks have been eroded, or worn away, by glacial action and running water. Today, many peaks have rounded tops, called "balds." Some are covered with grass, while others have masses of rhododendron, azalea, and laurel bushes that bloom in spring.

About 95 percent of the park is a magnificent forest that contains a larger variety of plants than any other North American forest. There are 130 kinds of trees, 1,600 flowering plants, 2,000 kinds of mushrooms, and more than 500 species of lichen and moss. Wildlife is also plentiful in the park. Nearly 250 kinds of birds have been officially recorded there.

In the early 1800s, long before the park was established, pioneers settled in the lower valleys and basins of the Smokies. The pioneers' cabins and barns have been restored at several locations, such as Cades Cove. There is also a mill that uses a waterwheel for power.

Name: Refers to the smoke-like mist that covers the valleys
Location: North Carolina and Tennessee
Established: 1934
Size: 520,976 acres
Highest point: 6,643 feet above sea level (Clingmans Dome)
Trails: More than 800 miles
Number of visitors: 9.1 million per year
Rank: most visited
Animals: Black bear, bobcat, eagle, hawk, owl, red fox, red wolf, vulture, white-tailed deer, woodpecker
Plants: Azalea and mountain laurel plants; chestnut, oak, Fraser fir, red spruce, and tulip trees
Fun fact: The Smokies are the salamander capital of the world, with 27 species living in the mountains.

Opposite page:
The rugged peaks of the Smoky Mountains have been worn down over 200 million years.

IL

IN

OH

WV

KY

MO

Mammoth Cave
National Park

VA

TN

NC

★ ★ ★ ★ ★ ★ ★ ★ ★ ★ ★ ★ ★ ★ ★ ★ ★ ★ ★

Mammoth Cave

The most extensive cave system in the world is found in Mammoth Cave National Park in central Kentucky. Here, over millions of years, river and rainwater seeped into cracks in the ground, washing away the limestone. The cracks widened, and eventually became the passages and caves of this vast and magical underground world.

No one knows how many underground passageways exist in Mammoth Cave. While more than 350 miles have been mapped, there are still more passages to be discovered.

Meanwhile, water continues to erode the rock walls and enlarge the passageways. In some areas of the cave, stalactites, which look like icicles, hang from the ceiling. In other places, stalagmites, which also look like icicles, stick up from the floor. These were formed over long periods of time as water evaporated leaving behind these mineral formations. One of the more decorative features in the cave is called Frozen Niagara. It looks like a giant, white waterfall. In the Snowball Room, mineral clusters that look like snowballs have formed on the ceiling.

Scientists have discovered about 130 different animal species using Mammoth Cave. Some of these animals, such as eyeless fish and shrimp, spend their entire lives in the dark underground world.

The park also has interesting sights above ground. Cedar Sink is a deep sinkhole that formed when the roof of an underground passage collapsed. The cave's river comes out on one side of Cedar Sink, and then disappears into the ground on the other side.

Name: Refers to the huge ("mammoth") cave that is the centerpiece of the park
Location: Kentucky
Established: 1941
Size: 52,830 acres
Highest point: About 900 feet above sea level (Mammoth Cave Ridge)
Trails: 70 miles
Number of visitors: About 2 million per year
Rank: 10th most visited
Animals: Raccoon, squirrel, white-tailed deer, wild turkeys, woodchuck (above ground); bat, camelback cave cricket, cave shrimp, crayfish (underground)
Plants: Dogwood, maple, oak, redbud, sassafras, and tulip trees
Fun fact: For a short time, in the 1840s, there was a tuberculosis hospital in the caves.

Opposite page:
Stalactites create a "giant waterfall" in the cave's Frozen Niagara formation.

AMERICA'S TOP

10

NATIONAL PARKS

CANADA

Olympic
National
Park

WA

ID

OR

Olympic

★ ★ ★ ★ ★ ★ ★ ★ ★ ★ ★ ★ ★ ★ ★ ★ ★ ★ ★

Olympic National Park is located on the Olympic Peninsula in northwestern Washington. It has a unique mix of environments, from ocean beaches to rain forests to snow-capped mountains.

Temperate rain forests grow on the western slopes of the mountains to an altitude of about 1,000 feet. From 1,000 to about 5,000 feet there are drier forests. Above 5,000 feet is the cool alpine zone, where only mosses, lichens, and small flowering plants survive.

The park's western side receives an average of 150 inches of rain per year, which makes it one of the wettest places in North America. The heavy rainfall, together with water from the mountains, has helped to create dense jungles where tall evergreen trees shadow giant ferns and thick carpets of moss. The world's largest known specimens of western hemlock and western red cedar trees are also found in these forests.

Many of the park's mountains rise 7,000 feet or more. There are at least 60 glaciers near the summits. Mount Olympus—the park's highest mountain—has 7 glaciers. The largest is the beautiful Blue Glacier, which is about 3 miles long.

Along the Pacific Ocean is Ruby Beach, where the sand often appears reddish in color. It actually contains large amounts of tiny crystals of the red gemstone garnet.

One of the main reasons that the park was created was to protect the Roosevelt elk. This member of the deer family can stand 8 feet high at the shoulder and weigh almost 1,000 pounds. Some herds remain at the park year-round.

Name: Mount Olympus and the Olympic Peninsula on which the park is located are named after the mythical home of Greek gods.
Location: Washington
Established: 1938
Size: 922,651 acres
Highest point: 7,965 feet above sea level (Mount Olympus)
Trails: Over 600 miles
Number of visitors: 4.7 million per year
Rank: 3rd most visited
Animals: Bald eagle, black bear, black-tailed deer, cormorant, Olympic marmot, Roosevelt elk, seal, sea lion, spotted owl
Plants: Douglas fir, Sitka spruce, western hemlock, and western red cedar trees
Fun fact: There are 5 animal species and 8 plant types found only on the peninsula.

Opposite page:
Layers of snow glisten atop a mountain in Olympic National Park.

AMERICA'S TOP

10

NATIONAL PARKS

WY
NE
UT
★
Rocky Mountain
National Park
CO
KS
AZ
NM
OK

Rocky Mountain

★ ★ ★ ★ ★ ★ ★ ★ ★ ★ ★ ★ ★ ★ ★ ★ ★

Some of the most rugged mountain scenery in America is found in Rocky Mountain National Park. Except for a few roads, the wilderness there is almost completely undisturbed.

The park has 65 mountain peaks that are 10,000 feet or higher. Many of these are covered with snow year-round. There are glaciers on some of the west-facing slopes.

Trail Ridge Road, the highest paved road in the United States, crosses Rocky Mountain National Park from east to west. Its highest point is at 12,183 feet. No trees grow above 11,500 feet. Instead, there is tundra—flat land with a cold climate and a short growing season. The vegetation that survives in these conditions is the same as that found in the Arctic.

Running along the crest of the Rockies is the Continental Divide, the "backbone" of North America. This imaginary line divides land draining into east-flowing streams from land draining into west-flowing streams. Water flows down the eastern slopes toward the Atlantic Ocean and down the western slopes toward the Pacific Ocean.

In the sheltered valleys at the base of the Rockies are lakes and meadows. In early spring, when the snow melts, the wildflowers burst into colorful bloom. More than 700 types of flowering plants are found in the park. Wildlife is also abundant, particularly elk, mule deer, beaver, and the Rocky Mountain bighorn—wild sheep that move swiftly along the mountain ledges.

Name: Honors the mountain range in which the park is located
Location: Colorado
Established: 1915
Size: 265,727 acres
Highest point: 14,255 feet above sea level (Longs Peak)
Trails: 355 miles
Number of visitors: About 3 million per year
Rank: 7th most visited
Animals: Beaver, bighorn, elk, hawk, jay, mule deer, ptarmigan
Plants: Aspen, blue spruce, Engelmann spruce, limber pine, and lodgepole pine trees
Fun fact: At the base of Andrews Glacier is a lake that looks like milk because it contains powdered rock.

Opposite page:
Many of the park's rugged cliffs remain completely wild and undisturbed.

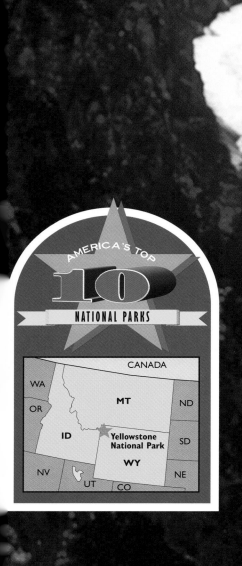

Yellowstone

★ ★ ★ ★ ★ ★ ★ ★ ★ ★ ★ ★ ★ ★ ★ ★ ★ ★

Yellowstone, the world's first national park, is best known for its geysers, which send hot water and steam shooting high into the air. Yellowstone has about 300 active geysers in addition to areas of hot, bubbling mud and vents where steam escapes from underground.

The most famous geyser at Yellowstone is Old Faithful. This geyser erupts on a more-or-less regular schedule, although it has slowed down over time. Today it averages about 1 eruption every 77 minutes. Each time Old Faithful erupts, it shoots 12,000 gallons of water up to heights of between 106 and 184 feet.

As the hot water from Old Faithful and the other geysers rises to the earth's surface, it carries various minerals, which are left on the ground after the water evaporates. At Mammoth Hot Springs there are terraces created by white limestone deposits. Elsewhere, sulfur deposits leave a yellow coating on the ground.

Some of the park's most spectacular scenery can be seen along the Yellowstone River. At the southern end are two large waterfalls—Upper Falls, which drops 109 feet, and Lower Falls, which has a 308-foot drop. The rushing river has cut a canyon into the rocks that is over 1,000 feet deep and 24 miles long. This canyon is known as Yellowstone's Grand Canyon.

Another beautiful spot is Yellowstone Lake—North America's largest mountain lake. There, bison come to drink, and pelicans swoop down to catch fish in their large bills.

Name: Refers to Yellowstone River in the southeastern part of park
Location: Wyoming, Montana, and Idaho
Established: 1872
Size: 2.2 million acres
Highest point: 11,358 feet above sea level (Eagle Peak)
Trails: About 1,200 miles
Number of visitors: 3.1 million per year
Rank: 6th most visited
Animals: Bison, black bear, deer, elk, pelican, wolf
Plants: Douglas fir, lodgepole pine, spruce, and whitebark pine trees
Fun fact: One place where mud bubbles explosively at the earth's surface is called Dragon's Mouth.

Opposite page:
The Yellowstone River gushes over Lower Falls and through Yellowstone's Grand Canyon.

AMERICA'S TOP

10

NATIONAL PARKS

OR   ID

CA

NV   UT

Pacific Ocean

Yosemite
National
Park

AZ

MEXICO

Yosemite

★ ★ ★ ★ ★ ★ ★ ★ ★ ★ ★ ★ ★ ★ ★ ★ ★

Some of the world's most famous natural scenery is found in Yosemite National Park. The park was established to preserve the giant sequoia trees in the area and Yosemite Falls—one of the world's highest waterfalls.

The centerpiece of the park is Yosemite Valley. Surrounded by the Merced River, this flat, meadow-like valley is about 7 miles long and 1 mile wide. Sheer granite mountains rise almost straight up from both sides of the valley. Besides Yosemite, there are waterfalls that come roaring to life in the spring, when snow melts on the mountains. Ribbon Falls drops 1,612 feet straight down—a distance 9 times greater than that of Niagara Falls. Yosemite Falls, which actually consists of 3 waterfalls—one above the other—has a total drop of 2,425 feet.

At the lower end of Yosemite Valley is El Capitan, the largest block of granite on the earth. Its sheer walls rise up 3,593 feet. At the upper end of the valley is Half Dome, a 4,733-foot-high mountain that looks as if its northern face has been cut away.

The park is famous for its 3 groves of giant sequoias—among the largest trees in the world. Some of Yosemite's sequoias stand more than 200 feet tall and have bases over 30 feet in diameter. Most of the trees are 2,500 to 3,000 years old.

The Sierra Nevada range covers more than 90 percent of Yosemite. Here, there are towering mountains, such as Mount Lyell and Cathedral Peak, as well as Tuolumne Meadows, a large grassland 8,600 feet above sea level.

Name: Derived from yo'hem-iteh, a name for the Native Americans who once lived in the valley. The name means "grizzly bear," which was the Native Americans' totem (a natural object or animal used as a group's emblem).
Location: California
Established: 1890
Size: 747,956 acres
Highest point: 13,114 feet above sea level (Mount Lyell)
Trails: 840 miles
Number of visitors: 4.1 million per year
Rank: 4th most visited
Animals: Acorn woodpecker, black bear, coyote, jay, mountain lion, peregrine falcon, ringtail cat
Plants: Fir, oak, pine, and sequoia trees
Fun fact: Some 60,000 people see the park each year on horseback.

Opposite page:
Ice-covered rocks are part of the mystical landscape in Yosemite Valley.

AMERICA'S TOP

10

NATIONAL PARKS

ID

WY

NV

UT

Zion
National
Park

CO

AZ

Zion

★ ★ ★ ★ ★ ★ ★ ★ ★ ★ ★ ★ ★ ★ ★ ★ ★ ★

The land on which Zion National Park is now located was formed over millions of years. Its rock formations, steep gorges, and colorful canyons reveal a fascinating geological history. Before the Age of Dinosaurs, this land was covered by an ocean. For millions of years, the rocks have been eroded (worn away) by wind and water.

Erosion has shaped the rocks in wonderful ways, creating huge arches, pillars, and even a throne. One of the park's main features is Zion Canyon, a deep, narrow canyon formed by the Virgin River. The cliffs on both sides display many shades of red, orange, pink, purple, and cream. From early morning until sunset, the shifting light falls on the canyon, changing the colors of the rocks.

One of the park's cliffs is called Weeping Rock. There, water from an underground source comes to the surface and drips slowly, creating an oasis in this desert environment. Flowering plants and ferns that grow on the cliff are moistened year-round by the dripping water. Among the animals living in this beautiful hanging garden is the Zion snail. This small creature—less than 1/4 inch in diameter—is found nowhere else in the world.

Some of the best views of the park can be seen along the famous Zion–Mount Carmel Road. The road climbs steeply for 3 miles and takes many sharp turns. It then goes into a canyon wall, passing through a tunnel that is more than a mile long. The tunnel has 6 windows for viewing the majestic scenery.

Name: Zion means "place of peace and tranquility."
Location: Utah
Established: 1909
Size: 147,035 acres
Highest point: 8,826 feet above sea level (Horse Pasture Mountain)
Trails: 122 miles
Number of visitors: 2.4 million per year
Rank: 9th most visited
Animals: Bighorn sheep, lizard, mountain lion, mule deer, peregrine falcon, songbird, squirrel
Plants: Box elder, cottonwood, Douglas fir, ponderosa pine trees
Fun fact: The world's largest natural arch is found there—Kolob Arch— with a span of 310 feet.

Opposite page: Unusual rock formations are a distinctive feature of Zion National Park.

America's Top 10 National Parks are not necessarily the "best" national parks, but they receive the most visitors. Below is a complete list of the national parks in the United States.

America's National Parks

Name	Location	Name	Location
Acadia	Maine	Isle Royale	Michigan
Arches	Utah	Joshua Tree	California
Badlands	South Dakota	Katmai	Alaska
Big Bend	Texas	Kenai Fjords	Alaska
Biscayne	Florida	Kings Canyon	California
Bryce Canyon	Utah	Kobuk Valley	Alaska
Canyonlands	Utah	Lake Clark	Alaska
Capitol Reef	Utah	Lassen Volcanic	California
Carlsbad Caverns	New Mexico	Mammoth Cave	Kentucky
Channel Islands	California	Mesa Verde	Colorado
Crater Lake	Oregon	Mount Rainier	Washington
Death Valley	California and Nevada	North Cascades	Washington
		Olympic	Washington
Denali	Alaska	Petrified Forest	Arizona
Dry Tortugas	Florida	Redwood	California
Everglades	Florida	Rocky Mountain	Colorado
Gates of the Arctic	Alaska	Saguaro	Arizona
Glacier	Montana	Sequoia	California
Glacier Bay	Alaska	Shenandoah	Virginia
Grand Canyon	Arizona	Theodore Roosevelt	North Dakota
Grand Teton	Wyoming	Virgin Island	U.S. Virgin Islands
Great Basin	Nevada	Voyageurs	Minnesota
Great Smoky Mountain	North Carolina and Tennessee	Wind Cave	South Dakota
		Wrangell–St. Elias	Alaska
Guadalupe Mountains	Texas	Yellowstone	Montana, Wyoming, and Idaho
Haleakala	Hawaii		
Hawaii Volcanoes	Hawaii	Yosemite	California
Hot Springs	Arkansas	Zion	Utah

See page 231 for more information about national parks.

AMERICA'S TOP

10

NATURAL WONDERS

AMERICA'S TOP

10

NATURAL WONDERS

MT

Devils Tower

ID   SD

WY

NE

UT   CO

★ ★ ★ ★ ★ ★ ★ ★ ★ ★ ★ ★ ★ ★ ★ ★ ★ ★ ★

Devils Tower

The movie *Close Encounters of the Third Kind* made the image of Devils Tower, in Wyoming, famous the world over. In the movie, the aliens landed their spaceship near this towering, 865-foot-tall rock column. Seen close up or from a distance, Devils Tower is grand, and also a little spooky, especially when the top part is surrounded by mist.

Devils Tower is the tallest rock formation of its type in America—it is even taller than most American skyscrapers. The massive rock column looms over the surrounding landscape like a pyramid built by some ancient group of giants. The Sioux called Devils Tower *Mato Tipila*, which means "bear's lodge." According to the Sioux's oral tradition, the Great Spirit built the tower to save 7 little girls from a giant bear. The vertical grooves in the rock were said to be claw marks made by the bear when it tried to reach the girls, who were at the top of the tower.

Scientists have a different explanation for how Devils Tower was created. About 53 million years ago, a solid mass of magma (liquid volcanic rock) deep within the earth was forced upward. It came to rest 2,000 feet below the surface. There, the magma cooled and split into vertical columns, which became the tower and the grooves. Erosion of the surrounding landscape eventually brought the rock tower to the earth's surface. Over time, ice in the crevices caused the stone to crack in places. Some of its columns broke off, and these massive blocks still lie in heaps at the base of Devils Tower.

Location: Wyoming
Type of wonder: Natural rock tower
Claim to fame: Tallest rock formation of its type in America
Outstanding features: Imposing size, height, flattened top
Number of visitors: 450,000 per year
Dimensions: Base 1,000 feet in diameter; top 300 feet north to south, 180 feet east to west
Fun fact: About 5,000 people climb the tower each year.

Opposite page:
Devils Tower looms over
the flat Wyoming landscape.

AMERICA'S TOP

10

NATURAL WONDERS

OR   ID

Giant
Redwoods
        NV
            UT
    CA
Pacific Ocean
        AZ
    MEXICO

Giant Redwoods

In 1963, the world's tallest tree was discovered on the banks of a creek in northern California by the National Geographic Society. The Tall Tree as it is called, is a coast redwood. As a group, these redwoods grow taller than any other trees on earth. When it was first found, the Tall Tree stood 368 feet above the ground—taller than a football field is long!

In 1995, the Tall Tree lost its title to a nearby redwood called the National Geographic Society Tree. This redwood was discovered at the same time as the Tall Tree, but measured only 366 feet high. It is "taller" than the Tall Tree, because silt has built up around the Tall Tree's base, which has decreased its height above the ground. Since 1995, other taller trees have been discovered and the Tall Tree now ranks 11th tallest in the world.

Coast redwoods only grow along the Pacific Coast of America, from southern Oregon to the San Francisco area. The only other living redwoods are the dawn redwood, found in China, and the Giant Sequoias, found in the Sierra Nevada Mountains. In prehistoric times, however, redwoods grew in many parts of the world. Their fossils date back 100 million years. The Tall Tree is around 600 years old and may continue to grow for many years. Although the average age of coast redwoods is 500 to 700 years, some are as old as 2,000 years.

These giant redwoods originated either from tiny seeds or from growths, called "burls," at the bases of adult trees. The two tall trees stand in California's Redwood National Park.

Location: Redwood National Park, California

Type of wonder: Giant trees

Claim to fame: Among the tallest trees on earth

Outstanding features: Towering, tapering trunks with crowns that seem to reach the sky

Number of visitors: 552,500 per year

Dimensions: The Tall Tree is 14 feet in diameter; the National Geographic Tree is 14.1 feet in diameter

Fun fact: A redwood seed is only 3 times the size of a pinhead.

Opposite page:
Coast redwoods are known for their great height.

AMERICA'S TOP

10

NATURAL WONDERS

AK

CANADA

Glacier Bay

Glacier Bay

★ ★ ★ ★ ★ ★ ★ ★ ★ ★ ★ ★ ★ ★ ★ ★ ★ ★

Glacier Bay extends some 60 miles into Alaska from the Pacific Ocean. From the bay, narrow inlets that look like fingers cut into the mountainous back country. Some of the glaciers that cover these mountains reach as far as the inlets. These "tidewater" glaciers end as towering, solid walls of ice, some of which are 265 feet high. They produce immense icebergs by a process called "calving." This is believed to occur when water seeps under a glacier, melting and lifting it from the underlying rock. Pieces of the ice wall then break off. With a great rumble, the jagged chunks of ice crash into the water and float out to sea. Calving can be seen easily from the water, but for safety reasons, boats don't get too close to the massive walls of ice.

Some glaciers, such as the Johns Hopkins Glacier, are slowly moving forward into the water. Glaciers advance in shallow water, and can move up to 2 miles in 100 years. When moving forward into deeper water, glaciers bulldoze the rocks in front of them. They also melt, which makes them appear to be moving backwards. The famous Muir Glacier has retreated as much as 5 miles in 10 years. The bay's advancing glaciers originate high in the mountains—about 6,500 feet above sea level—while the retreating, or melting glaciers begin at altitudes only half as high.

Glacier Bay was established as a national monument in 1925 to protect its magnificent scenery and wildlife, which ranges from mountain goats to killer whales.

Location: Alaska
Type of wonder: Tidewater glaciers
Claim to fame: Calving of icebergs into the sea
Outstanding features: Huge ice walls, icebergs crashing into the water, mountain scenery
Number of visitors: 252,300 per year
Dimensions: The wall of the Muir Glacier is about 265 feet high (above water), and almost 2 miles wide.
Fun fact: The Muir Glacier has retreated more than 25 miles since 1890.

Opposite page:
Like a giant river of ice, this glacier dwarfs a passing cruise ship.

AMERICA'S TOP

10

NATURAL WONDERS

NV   UT   CO

★ Grand
Canyon

CA

AZ

NM

MEXICO

★ ★ ★ ★ ★ ★ ★ ★ ★ ★ ★ ★ ★ ★ ★ ★ ★ ★ ★ ★

Grand Canyon

The Grand Canyon is the world's most dramatic example of how water can erode, or wear away, the earth's surface. This place of awesome beauty, with its rugged walls of red, gray, and cream-colored rock, was carved out of the landscape by the Colorado River. The size of the canyon is monumental—277 miles long, more than 1 mile deep, and up to 18 miles wide. The South Rim is 7,000 feet high, and the North Rim rises as much as 9,000 feet from the canyon floor. Because of this change in altitude, the floor and the rim of the canyon have very different climates. On the floor of the canyon is a hot desert, while along the North Rim is a cool, wet forest. During the winter, the North Rim is blanketed by snow—as much as 200 inches.

For geologists (scientists who study the physical history of the earth), the canyon walls provide a look back in time. The rocks at the bottom are 2 billion years old. These are the remains of ancient mountains and are among the oldest exposed rocks on earth. About 600 million years ago, these mountains had been worn down to a flat plain. Fossils show that the plain was once covered by a sea and later by a desert.

The Grand Canyon as it exists today began taking shape about 10 million years ago. After the Colorado River was formed, it began flowing downhill from high in the Rocky Mountains, crossing the Colorado Plateau. Over the centuries, rocks, sand, and pebbles carried by the rushing water wore away the stone of the plateau, creating a landscape of great beauty and wonder.

Location: Arizona
Type of wonder: Rock canyon
Claim to fame: Immense size and a 2-billion-year record of earth's history
Outstanding features: Towering walls, cliffs, rocky formations, and a cross-section of the earth's surface
Number of visitors: 4.6 million per year
Dimensions: Total area is 1,904 square miles
Fun fact: Sharks' teeth that are 250 million years old have been found in the canyon's rocks.

Opposite page:
The canyon's beautiful rock layers reveal the changes that have occurred in the earth's surface over the last 2 billion years.

AMERICA'S TOP

10

NATURAL WONDERS

OH
IN
IL
WV
KY
VA
★ Mammoth
Cave
TN
NC

Mammoth Cave

Kentucky's Mammoth Cave is 350 miles long. It is the longest cave system in the world. Scientists believe that not all of this vast underground world has been discovered. The cave is a maze of passages, towering rooms, and deep pits. Everywhere, beautiful formations of rock resemble waterfalls, draperies, flowers, and coral. In some places, formations called stalactites, which look like rock icicles, hang from the cave roof. Formations called stalagmites stick up from the floor.

Mammoth Cave began taking shape more than 200 million years ago. For millions of years, river and rainwater seeped into cracks in the ground, dissolving the limestone. The cracks gradually widened and enlarged to form miles of underground rooms and passages. One room, called Mammoth Dome, has a 192-foot-high ceiling! There is also a 105-foot-deep pit, known as the Bottomless Pit.

People have been visiting Mammoth Cave for thousands of years. Prehistoric tools have been found there. The first tourists began coming to the cave in 1816. Today, about half a million people visit the cave each year.

More than 130 animal species either live in or spend time within the lightless world of Mammoth Cave. Some of these creatures, such as bats and crickets, regularly leave the cave to hunt for food. Others exist in darkness and never leave. Many of these animals, like the crayfish, are eyeless and colorless. Neither feature is necessary for creatures who live in a world darker than the blackest night.

Location: Kentucky
Type of wonder: Cave
Claim to fame: World's longest cave system
Outstanding features: Beautiful rock formations, deep pits, endless passages
Number of visitors: 500,000 per year
Dimensions: 350 miles long
Fun fact: Nitrate (used to make gunpowder) was mined at Mammoth Cave during the War of 1812.

Opposite page:
Massive stalactites hang from the ceiling of Mammoth Cave.

AMERICA'S TOP

10

NATURAL WONDERS

NV   UT   CO

CA   Meteor
      Crater ★

      AZ   NM

MEXICO

Meteor Crater

On a desert plain in northern Arizona lies a gigantic, bowl-shaped crater. It is 4,180 feet across and 560 feet deep. Its rim rises 160 feet above the surrounding land. Originally, this huge hole was believed to be a volcanic crater. In the 1890s, however, geologists discovered pieces of iron there. Iron is a major component of meteors (masses of stone or metal from outer space that reach the earth). This fact led Daniel Barringer, a mining engineer, to propose that the crater was produced by a huge meteor. A few years later, nickel, another element of meteors, was found in the crater's underlying soil. This discovery left little doubt that the crater was caused by the impact of an object from outer space.

Scientists suspect that the meteor that landed in the Arizona desert weighed several hundred thousand tons and was 150 feet in diameter. To make such a gigantic hole, the meteor was probably traveling at a speed of about 9 miles per second. Scientists also believe that the meteor exploded when it hit the earth. The force of that explosion was probably more than 100 times that of the atomic blast in Hiroshima, Japan, during World War II. The soil on the floor of the crater contains many different minerals, such as silica. These minerals were created from the desert sand by the intense heat and force of the explosion upon impact. Scientists suspect that the collision occurred as many as 50,000 years ago. Whenever it took place, the meteor strike in the Arizona desert must have been an earth-shaking event.

Location: Arizona desert
Type of wonder: Crater formed by a meteor
Claim to fame: Monstrous size
Outstanding features: A giant, bowl-shaped hole in the earth
Number of visitors: 300,000 per year
Dimensions: 4,180 feet across; 560 feet deep
Fun fact: There are about 30 craters on the earth caused by meteors.

Opposite page:
Scientists suspect that this immense crater may have been made by a meteor that was 150 feet in diameter.

AMERICA'S TOP
10
NATURAL WONDERS

CANADA

NY

Niagara
Falls

ME
VT
NH
MA
CT RI
PA
NJ
MD

Niagara Falls

★ ★ ★ ★ ★ ★ ★ ★ ★ ★ ★ ★ ★ ★ ★ ★ ★ ★ ★ ★

Niagara Falls, on the border of New York State and Ontario, Canada, is considered America's most magnificent waterfall. Several American waterfalls are larger, but none are as spectacular. The average amount of water flowing down the Niagara River is 212,000 cubic feet per second. Although less than half this amount actually goes over the falls—the rest is redirected to an electrical power plant—the sound of the falling water is thunderous. In fact, the name *Niagara* comes from a Neutre Native-American word that means "thundering waters."

Niagara actually consists of 3 waterfalls. On the American side lie the American Falls and the narrow Bridal Veil Falls. These are separated by the small Luna Island. Horseshoe Falls, along the Canadian border, is separated from the American Falls by Goat Island. Together, the 2 American falls drop 190 feet and are 2,400 feet across. Horseshoe Falls is 185 feet high and 3,600 feet across.

When Niagara Falls was first formed it was only 1 falls and was located 7 miles downstream from its present site. The falls were created at the end of the last Ice Age, about 12,000 years ago. Near Lake Ontario, the river flowed over a limestone cliff and began dissolving the limestone. Eventually, the limestone caved in, and Niagara Falls was born. As the water continued to erode the cliff, the falls shifted further upstream and split into 3 falls. Scientists believe that in 25,000 years, the falls will reach Lake Erie and become rapids.

Location: Border of New York State and Canada's province of Ontario

Type of wonder: Waterfall

Claim to fame: America's largest and most powerful waterfall

Outstanding feature: Massive wall of thundering water

Number of visitors: 14–15 million per year

Dimensions: Together, the American falls are 190 feet high and 2,400 feet across; Horseshoe Falls is 185 feet high and 3,600 feet across.

Fun fact: In 1901, Annie Edson Taylor was the first person to go over Horseshoe Falls in a barrel alive.

Opposite page:
Tourists get a closer look at the thundering waters of Niagara.

AMERICA'S TOP

10

NATURAL WONDERS

MT

★ Old Faithful

ID

SD

WY

NE

UT

CO

Old Faithful

Old Faithful is one of the world's most famous geysers. It is one of more than 300 geysers in Yellowstone National Park, which has the largest concentration of hot springs in the world. (Geysers are a type of hot spring.) Few geysers erupt as regularly as Old Faithful, which spouts almost hourly every day of the year. This predictable behavior, along with its 130-foot-high plume of steam and spray, have contributed to the geyser's fame.

Actually, Old Faithful is not as regular as most people believe. Over the years, the interval between eruptions has varied from 32 minutes to 2 hours. Calculations show, however, that it spouts about once every hour. For many years, the average interval was 65 minutes. Little by little, this time increased to 69 minutes. After an earthquake in 1983, eruptions began occurring about every 77 minutes.

The reason why there are so many geysers and other hot springs in Yellowstone is because millions of years ago, the region experienced a large amount of volcanic activity. Molten rock accumulated below ground, and when surface water collects there, it is heated by the volcanic rock. Where there is enough pressure on the heated water, its temperature is raised above the normal boiling point, but it does not begin to evaporate. The water can reach temperatures of up to 400° Fahrenheit before it finally turns to steam. At that point it is released explosively through an opening in the earth's surface. It is this impressive and dramatic display that draws millions to Old Faithful each year.

Location: Yellowstone National Park, Wyoming

Type of wonder: Geyser

Claim to fame: Erupts almost hourly every day of the year

Outstanding features: A regularly occurring fountain of steam and hot water, over 130 feet high

Number of visitors: 3.1 million per year

Dimensions: Plume of steam and spray rises 130 feet above ground

Fun fact: Each eruption is signaled by a splash of water above Old Faithful's crater.

Opposite page:
Old Faithful erupts about once every 77 minutes, spraying water 130 feet into the air.

ID
WY
NV
UT
CO
Rainbow
Bridge
AZ

Rainbow Bridge

★ ★ ★ ★ ★ ★ ★ ★ ★ ★ ★ ★ ★ ★ ★ ★ ★ ★ ★

Tucked in a remote canyon in southeast Utah, is a huge natural sandstone bridge. Its colors include orange, red, and brown, and according to Native-American legends, the bridge was a rainbow that turned to stone. Until early in the 20th century, only Native Americans had ever seen the bridge. In 1909, they guided a group of archaeologists and geologists into the Utah canyon, and the bridge became known to the rest of the world. Rainbow Bridge is still so remote that it is hard to reach by land. Most visitors who journey there take a boat from Lake Powell, and then must hike about half a mile to reach the bridge.

Rainbow Bridge is the world's largest known natural stone bridge. It arches 290 feet above the floor of the canyon and spans a distance of 275 feet. The stone at the top of the arch is 42 feet thick and 33 feet wide and could accommodate 2 lanes of traffic!

It took millions of years for nature to build Rainbow Bridge. The process began 60 million years ago, after the Colorado Plateau was formed. Bridge Creek, which flowed over the plateau, began cutting into the surface rock, exposing the underlying sandstone. Scientists believe that the bridge was once part of a narrow rock wall that stood in the canyon. The center of the wall was slowly eroded by water. This opening in the rock gradually widened, forming the bridge. It is still being enlarged by water erosion. In 1910, the U.S. government formally established the bridge as the Rainbow Bridge National Monument.

Location: Southeast Utah
Type of wonder: Natural stone bridge
Claim to fame: World's largest natural bridge
Outstanding features: Huge span and height
Number of visitors: 346,200 per year
Dimensions: Span: 275 feet; height: 290 feet
Fun fact: The Capitol Building in Washington, D.C., could fit under the arch.

Opposite page:
The top of this massive bridge is wide enough to hold 2 lanes of traffic.

AMERICA'S TOP

10

NATURAL WONDERS

UT   CO   KS

OK

AZ

NM

White
Sands

TX

MEXICO

White Sands

White Sands looks like a skier's paradise, with its glistening wind-swept hills of snow-white powder. This powder is not snow, however, but gypsum, a special type of sand. White Sands in southern New Mexico is the largest gypsum dune field in the world. Gypsum is a mineral that is soluble, which means that it will dissolve in water, like salt or sugar.

The dune field lies in the Tularosa Basin between the San Andreas Mountains, and the Sacramento Mountains. White Sands covers an area of 275 square miles and is separated in places by flat ground. The gypsum that forms the dunes comes from the mountains. Rainwater dissolves the gypsum and carries it down the mountains into Lake Lucero, a seasonal lake. This lake is dry most of the year. When the winds are strong and steady, they deposit gypsum grains from the lake onto the dunes of White Sands. New dunes are constantly being formed as they drift northeastward.

The shifting sands and dry weather make it difficult for plants and animals to survive there. The soaptree yucca has adapted by spreading out its shallow roots to absorb dew from the desert's surface. Others have deep roots that tap the underlying water. Many different animals, such as coyotes and kangaroo rats, live on the edges of White Sands. Some species, such as the bleached earless lizard and the all-white Apache pocket mouse, have adapted to the unique environment. Like the sand, they are completely white.

Location: White Sands National Monument, New Mexico

Type of wonder: Sand dunes

Claim to fame: Largest deposit of gypsum on the earth's surface

Outstanding features: Vast landscape of snow-white sand, miles of shifting dunes

Number of visitors: 604,800 per year

Dimensions: About 275 square miles

Fun fact: Some of the plants growing in White Sands have 40-foot-long stems.

Opposite page:
For plants to survive in this harsh environment, they must grow faster than the sand rises, or they will be buried.

America's Top 10 Natural Wonders are not necessarily the "best," but we consider each of these wonders to be the best of its type. Below are 10 additional natural wonders.

More American Natural Wonders		
Name	Location	Description
Quechee Gorge	Vermont	Narrow ravine, 165 feet deep, cut by Ottauquechee River.
Palisades Cliffs	New York and New Jersey	14 miles of 150–530-foot-high rock cliffs long the Hudson River.
Carlsbad Caverns National Park	New Mexico	250-million-year-old limestone cave.
Sleeping Bear Dunes	Michigan	34-mile-long dunes towering 460 feet above Lake Michigan.
Badlands National Monument	South Dakota	Landscape of rock spires, towers, canyons, gorges.
Scotts Bluff National Monument	Nebraska	800-foot-high, 0.5-mile-long bluff over the North Platte Valley.
Petrified Forest National Park	Arizona	Fossilized trees from the Age of the Dinosaurs.
Bryce Canyon National Park	Utah	Basin in limestone, shale, and sandstone containing unusual and colorful rock formations.
Crater Lake National Park	Oregon	Brilliant blue lake in the crater of an ancient volcano; deepest in the United States at almost 2,000 feet.

Crater Lake

See page 232 for more information about natural wonders.

AMERICA'S TOP

10

RIVERS

AMERICA'S TOP

10

RIVERS

WY
NE
IA
CO
KS
KY
MO
NM
Arkansas River
AR
TN
OK
TX
LA
MS

The Arkansas River

★ ★ ★ ★ ★ ★ ★ ★ ★ ★ ★ ★ ★ ★ ★ ★ ★

The Arkansas River is one of the major tributaries (offshoots) of the Mississippi. It forms in the Rocky Mountains of central Colorado and flows eastward into Kansas. From Wichita, Kansas, the river turns southeast, flowing through Oklahoma and across central Arkansas. North of Arkansas City, the waters empty into the Mississippi.

The Arkansas descends more than 2 miles in elevation from source to mouth. Along the way, dams are used to provide flood control, crop irrigation, and electric power.

In Colorado, the river flows rapidly through the stunning Royal Gorge Canyon. The canyon's steep granite walls are spanned by the highest suspension bridge in America, the Royal Gorge Bridge. The Arkansas's rushing waters slow down at the Pueblo Reservoir. Visitors to this calm lake are surrounded by limestone cliffs and snow-capped mountain views.

In Kansas, the river widens and moves more slowly. It flows through prairies where millions of bison, or buffalo, once roamed. Today, these prairies are one of America's major wheat-producing regions. Corn and alfalfa also are raised here, thanks to irrigation water from the Arkansas. Cattle ranches are common on the prairies, too. Another important industry—petroleum—centers around the oil and natural gas fields found in the Arkansas River valley in Kansas and Oklahoma. The lower part of the river was widened in the early 1970s to allow barges and other boats to travel upstream as far as Tulsa, Oklahoma—the largest city on the river.

Name: From a Quapaw Indian word meaning "downstream people"

Location: Central United States

Length and rank: 1,459 miles; 4th longest

Source: Sawatch Range of the Rocky Mountains, Colorado

Flows into: Mississippi River

Major tributaries: Cimarron, Verdigris, and Canadian Rivers

Drainage area: 161,000 square miles

Major cities: Pueblo, CO; Wichita, KS; Tulsa, OK; Fort Smith and Little Rock, AR

Fun fact: In the late 1800s, legendary gunslingers Bat Masterson and Wyatt Earp were peace officers of Dodge City, Kansas, on the Arkansas River.

Opposite page:
The Arkansas provides water for many crops in the Arkansas River valley.

AMERICA'S TOP
10
RIVERS

NV
UT
WY
NE
CA
CO
Colorado River
AZ
NM
TX
MEXICO

The
Colorado River

★ ★ ★ ★ ★ ★ ★ ★ ★ ★ ★ ★ ★ ★

The Colorado River is the longest river west of the Rocky Mountains. It begins as a narrow stream in the Rocky Mountains in north-central Colorado. The river then flows southwest into Utah and northern Arizona and turns south, forming Arizona's borders with Nevada and California. Shortly after it passes Yuma, Arizona, the Colorado River enters Mexico. It empties into the Gulf of California, which is part of the Pacific Ocean.

The Colorado River has created some of the world's most spectacular scenery through the process of erosion (wearing away). For the past 6 million years, its flowing water has cut deep canyons into the rock. One of these is the Grand Canyon, which is 277 miles long, as much as 18 miles wide, and more than 1 mile deep.

The Colorado flows over more than 1,400 miles. Along the way, more than 50 rivers empty into it. Most of this water never reaches the Colorado's mouth because the water is used by cities and farmlands along the banks. Many dams have been built on the Colorado. The largest is Hoover Dam, on the border of Nevada and Arizona. Generators there provide electricity to Arizona, Nevada, and southern California.

In southern California, much of the Colorado's water is directed into the All-American Canal. About 80 miles long and 200 feet wide, this is the largest irrigation canal in the United States. It supplies water to the Imperial Valley, which was once desert. Today, citrus fruits, melons, cotton, and many other crops are grown there.

Name: From Spanish words meaning "reddish color"

Location: Southwestern United States and northern Mexico

Length and rank: 1,450 miles; 5th longest

Source: Rocky Mountain National Park, Colorado

Flows into: Gulf of California

Major U.S. tributaries: Gunnison, Dolores, Green, San Juan, Little Colorado, and Gila Rivers

Drainage area: 244,000 square miles

Major cities: Grand Junction, CO; Yuma, AZ

Fun fact: In 1996, an artificial flood was created where the Colorado River flows through the Grand Canyon to improve living conditions for rare fish, such as humpback chubs.

Opposite page:
The Colorado River has carved dramatic canyons in America's Southwest.

AMERICA'S TOP

10

RIVERS

CANADA

WA

Columbia River

OR

MI

ID

CA

NV

UT

CO

The
Columbia River

★ ★ ★ ★ ★ ★ ★   ★ ★ ★ ★ ★ ★ ★

The Columbia River starts at Columbia Lake, among the snow-capped Rocky Mountains in western Canada. It enters the United States in northeastern Washington and flows generally in a southerly direction to the Oregon border. It then flows west to the Pacific, forming the border between Washington and Oregon.

At one time, roaring rapids were common along the Columbia. The construction of numerous dams, however, has slowed the river. These dams provide electricity for homes and industries, water for irrigation, and protection against flooding. They also allow boats to travel more than 400 miles upriver from the mouth.

The largest of the dams is Grand Coulee, in northwestern Washington. One of the largest concrete structures in the world, it is 550 feet high and 5,223 feet long. Behind it, the Columbia widens to form Franklin D. Roosevelt Lake, which is 150 miles long.

The Bonneville Dam is on the Washington-Oregon Border. Visitors there can view fish ladders through underwater windows. A fish ladder consists of a series of pools alongside the dam. Each is slightly higher than the one below. They are designed to allow salmon to bypass the dam as they swim up the Columbia to their breeding grounds.

Before the dams were built and industries polluted the water, huge numbers of salmon swam in the Columbia. Now, to increase the population, young salmon are raised in fish hatcheries, and then released into the river.

Name: Named for his ship, "Columbia Rediviva," by the American trader Robert Gray, who explored the river's mouth in 1792

Location: Southwestern Canada and northwestern United States

Length and rank: 1,240 miles; 8th longest

Source: Columbia Lake, British Columbia, Canada

Flows into: Pacific Ocean

Major U.S. tributaries: Kootenay, Snake, and Willamette Rivers

Drainage area: 258,000 square miles

Major cities: Portland, OR; Vancouver, WA

Fun fact: In 1966, a salmon hatchery next to Bonneville Dam hatched 15 million salmon. About 1 percent of the fish survived to adulthood.

Opposite page:
The Columbia River flows through the beautiful landscape of the Pacific Northwest.

AMERICA'S TOP

10

RIVERS

MT ND CANADA
WY SD MN WI MI NY
NE IA IL IN OH PA
CO KS MO KY WV VA
Mississippi River
NM OK AR TN NC
SC
TX MS AL GA
LA FL
MEXICO

The
Mississippi River

The "Mighty Mississippi" is America's main river drainage system. Rivers in 31 states are connected to it, either directly or indirectly. All together, the Mississippi River system drains water from about 40 percent of the United States as well as parts of central Canada.

The Mississippi begins at Lake Itasca, Minnesota. There it is only about 12 feet wide and 1.5 feet deep. As the river flows south and is joined by tributaries, it grows wider and deeper—up to 5,000 feet wide and 12 feet deep. The lower part of the river meanders, or bends continuously. As a result, the length of the river between Cairo, Illinois, and New Orleans, Louisiana, is almost 3 times that of the valley.

The Mississippi carries huge amounts of sediment. The river bottom is constantly dredged (cleared) to remove this sediment and maintain a channel deep enough for navigation. As the river empties into the Gulf of Mexico, it deposits the sediment. Over thousands of years, this sediment has created fertile new land, called a delta.

In the spring, when snow melts and rainfall is heavy, the quantity of water carried by the Mississippi increases dramatically. To protect the surrounding towns against flooding, many dams and levees have been built along the river. This protection is not always enough, however. In the Great Flood of 1993, the river rose so high that it burst through the dams and levees. The floodwaters caused enormous damage to local crops and property.

Name: From an Algonquian Indian word meaning "father of waters"

Location: Central United States

Length and rank: 2,340 miles; longest

Source: Lake Itasca, Minnesota

Flows into: Gulf of Mexico

Major tributaries: Iowa, Des Moines, Illinois, Missouri, Ohio, St. Francis, Arkansas and Red Rivers

Drainage area: 1.2 million square miles

Major cities: Minneapolis—Saint Paul, MN; Saint Louis, MO; Cairo, IL; Memphis, TN; Natchez, MS; Baton Rouge and New Orleans, LA

Fun fact: Tourists enjoy riding on replicas of the steamboats that carried passengers along the river in the late 19th century.

Opposite page:
Barges travel up and down the wide Mississippi.

AMERICA'S TOP

10

RIVERS

The
Missouri River

★ ★ ★ ★ ★ ★ ★   ★ ★ ★ ★ ★ ★ ★

The "Mighty Mo" is the largest tributary of the Mississippi River. It originates at Three Forks, Montana, where the Jefferson, Gallatin, and Madison Rivers join together. The Missouri flows 2,714 miles from the Rocky Mountains to the Mississippi. On its journey, it flows through, or runs along the borders of, 7 states: Montana, North Dakota, South Dakota, Nebraska, Iowa, Kansas, and Missouri.

Near its source, the Missouri flows through mountainous terrain covered with evergreen forests where bear, elk, and moose live. Outside Helena, Montana, it flows through the deep, scenic gorge, Gates of the Mountains. Soon after, the river tumbles over a series of waterfalls, dropping 400 feet in 12 miles. Then the river broadens, its volume increased by water from many tributaries.

For most of its length, the Missouri flows through the Great Plains. Cattle and grain crops are raised in the fertile soil near the river. Trees such as poplar and hickory are common.

Dams built on the river have created several huge lakes, including Fort Peck Reservoir in Montana and Lake Sakakawea in North Dakota. These dams are used to control flooding, generate electricity, irrigate farmland, and provide recreation.

The Missouri has always been used for transportation. Native Americans traveled the river in canoes to trade with one another. Today, river traffic includes many tugboats pushing barges that carry grain, oil, and other products.

Name: From an Illinois Native American word meaning "dwellers of the big muddy"

Location: Central United States

Length and rank: 2,315 miles; 2nd longest

Source: Jefferson, Madison, and Gallatin Rivers

Flows into: Mississippi River

Major tributaries: Little Missouri, Cheyenne, James, Platte, and Kansas Rivers

Drainage area: 592,000 square miles

Major cities: Great Falls, MT; Bismarck, ND; Pierre, SD; Sioux City, IA; Omaha, NE; Kansas City, KS; Jefferson City, MO; and Saint Louis, MO

Fun fact: The Missouri carries so much sediment that people have nicknamed it Big Muddy.

Opposite page:
South Dakota's rolling hills are part of the scenery along the Missouri River.

AMERICA'S TOP

10

RIVERS

Ohio River

WI | MI | CANADA | NY
IL | IN | OH | PA
| | WV | VA
| KY | |
TN | | NC

The
Ohio River

★ ★ ★ ★ ★ ★ ★ ★ ★ ★ ★ ★ ★ ★ ★

The Ohio River starts in the middle of Pittsburgh, Pennsylvania, where it is surrounded by skyscrapers. There, the Allegheny and Monongahela Rivers come together at Point State Park. A giant fountain in the park symbolizes the joining of the two rivers to form the Ohio.

The Ohio River generally flows southwest, running along the borders of West Virginia, Ohio, Kentucky, Indiana, and Illinois. It joins the Mississippi River at Cairo, Illinois. The Ohio is the largest eastern tributary of the Mississippi.

The river is lined by steep bluffs for most of its length. In some places, beautiful forests of oak, hickory, and maple grow along the banks. White-tailed deer, squirrels, and pheasants populate these forests.

The river's upper valley is home to many industries. Soap, ceramics, and home appliances are among the many products manufactured there. The lower valley is dotted with farms where corn, soybeans, and tobacco are grown.

In Louisville, Kentucky, are the attractive rapids known as the Falls of the Ohio. Here, the river's elevation drops almost 24 feet in 2.5 miles. A canal was built around the rapids in 1830, allowing boats to move up and down the river.

The entire Ohio is navigable, thanks to dams and locks. Most of the river traffic consists of barges carrying coal that is mined nearby. All the states along the Ohio have coal mines. The coal is taken to power plants, where it is burned to produce electricity.

Name: From the Iroquois words meaning "beautiful river"

Location: East-central United States

Length and rank: 981 miles; 10th longest

Source: Allegheny and Monongahela Rivers in Pittsburgh, Pennsylvania

Flows into: Mississippi River

Major tributaries: Beaver, Scioto, Kentucky, Green, Wabash, and Tennessee Rivers

Drainage area: 203,000 square miles

Major cities: Pittsburgh, PA; Cincinnati, OH; Louisville, KY; Evansville, IN; and Paducah, KY

Fun fact: The city of Louisville, Kentucky, on the banks of the Ohio, is the original home of the famous Louisville Slugger baseball bats.

Opposite page:
The bright lights of Cincinnati's waterfront glitter on the Ohio River.

AMERICA'S TOP
10
RIVERS

OK
AR
Red River
TX
MS
LA

The Red River

The Red River forms much of the border between Oklahoma and Texas as well as part of the border between Texas and Arkansas. It flows southeast through Louisiana. About 11 miles before it joins the Mississippi, it divides into two rivers, called the Old River and the Atchafalaya River. The Old River flows into the Mississippi. The Atchafalaya flows south, emptying into the Gulf of Mexico. The Red can be navigated from the Gulf as far inland as Fulton, Arkansas.

The Red River system begins with Tierra Blanca Creek in eastern New Mexico. Hundreds of miles to the east, the creek's waters mingle with those of other creeks and rivers to form Prairie Dog Town Fork. In Oklahoma, this river merges with the North Fork Red River and becomes the Red River. The Red River flows through rolling plains of red clay, which gives the water its color—and the river its name.

Dams on the river protect the nearby land against flooding and provide water for irrigation. Along the Texas-Oklahoma border, much of the Red River valley is used for raising cattle and for growing wheat.

Lake Texoma, formed by Denison Dam, is about 70 miles north of Dallas. Other popular lakes are found in Louisiana, where the Red River's changing course has created cutoff lakes in the soft soil. These lakes often start out as U-shaped loops called "oxbows." When separated from the river—perhaps because the river has found another path—oxbows become cutoff lakes.

Name: From the water's reddish color

Location: South-central United States

Length and rank: 1,018 miles; 6th longest

Source: North Fork Red River and Prairie Dog Town Fork

Flows into: Mississippi and Atchafalaya Rivers

Major tributaries: Pease, Wichita, Tashita, Kiamichi, and Sulphur Rivers

Drainage area: 93,200 square miles

Major cities: Shreveport, LA; Alexandria, LA

Fun fact: The Red River valley in Louisiana is a major cotton-growing region.

Opposite page:
The red clay soil over which the river flows colors the water.

AMERICA'S TOP

10

RIVERS

UT CO KS MO

AZ NM OK AR

TX MS

Rio Grande LA

MEXICO

The Rio Grande River

The Rio Grande begins at an elevation of more than 12,000 feet in the mountains of southwestern Colorado. It tumbles downward as it travels eastward to Alamosa, Colorado. There, it turns south and flows through New Mexico to Texas, where it forms the border between Texas and Mexico. It then empties into the Gulf of Mexico.

The river has cut deep canyons in the flatlands of New Mexico. Rio Grande Gorge is 50 miles long and 800 feet deep. The walls of the gorge rise almost vertically from the river's edge. Further south is Bosque del Apache National Wildlife Refuge, home to many bobcats, deer, coyotes, and other wild animals. Many migrating birds spend the winter there—or use the refuge as a stopping place before continuing on their journey farther south.

From El Paso, in the westernmost part of Texas, to the Gulf of Mexico, the Rio Grande is an international waterway. Bridges connect cities in Texas with sister communities in Mexico. Americans and Mexicans alike enjoy the Amistad Reservoir, west of Del Rio, Texas. Overlooking the dam that forms this lake is a huge stone statue of Tlaloc, the Aztec rain god.

During most of the year, the Rio Grande carries little water. It has been dammed in many places to provide electricity, flood control, and water for irrigation. Farming is important in much of the Rio Grande valley. In southern New Mexico, crops such as pecans, cotton, onions, and lettuce are grown.

Name: Spanish for "great river"

Location: Southwestern United States and northern Mexico

Length and rank: 1,885 miles; 3rd longest

Source: Rocky Mountains in western Colorado

Flows into: Gulf of Mexico

Major U.S. tributaries: Chama, Puerco, Pecos, and Devils Rivers

Drainage area: 172,000 square miles

Major U.S. cities: Albuquerque, NM; El Paso, Laredo, and Brownsville, TX

Fun fact: In Mexico, this river is called Rio Bravo, meaning "brave river."

Opposite page:
The Rio Grande flows through the arid Texas desert.

The
Snake River

★ ★ ★ ★ ★ ★ ★   ★ ★ ★ ★ ★ ★

The Snake River originates in Yellowstone National Park. From there, it twists and turns through Wyoming, Idaho, Oregon, and Washington. Near Pasco, Washington, it empties into the Columbia River. The Snake River is the largest tributary of the Columbia.

Soon after the Snake leaves Yellowstone, it flows through Grand Teton National Park. There, it widens and forms Jackson Lake. Evergreen forests and colorful wildflower meadows line the banks of the lake.

In southeastern Idaho, the Snake River has cut a deep valley in the earth, forming steep canyons and many rapids and waterfalls. Among the most beautiful of these is Shoshone Falls, where the river plunges 212 feet over a horseshoe-shaped rim that is 900 feet wide.

As the Snake River crosses southern Idaho, it provides water for the famous Idaho potatoes, as well as for beans, wheat, and other crops. At the western side of the state, the Snake suddenly turns northward, forming much of the border between Idaho and Oregon. There, it flows through the 100-mile-long Hells Canyon—the deepest river gorge in the nation. With a depth of 7,900 feet, it is some 1,500 feet deeper than the Grand Canyon!

At Lewiston, Idaho, the Snake turns towards the west, flowing through southeastern Washington, where it is regulated by dams. To the river's north is a large wheat-growing area. The Snake is also a popular river for fishing. It is filled with many fish varieties, especially salmon.

Name: Named by European settlers who misinterpreted Shoshone sign language for "fish" to mean "snake."
Location: Northwestern United States
Length and rank: 1,040 miles; 9th longest
Source: Yellowstone National Park, Wyoming
Flows into: Columbia River
Major tributaries: Wind, Bruneau, Salmon, Powder, Clearwater, and Palouse Rivers
Drainage area: 108,000 square miles
Major cities: Idaho Falls and Lewiston, ID
Fun fact: The Snake River was used by pioneers traveling the Oregon Trail.

Opposite page:
The Snake River travels through many canyons on its journey from Wyoming to Washington.

AMERICA'S TOP

10

RIVERS

AK

CANADA

Yukon River

The
Yukon River

The Yukon begins in mountains in Yukon Territory and British Columbia. It flows northwest to Fort Yukon, Alaska. Then it flows in a southwesterly direction across a broad, tree-covered plain towards the Bering Sea. The river carries enormous amounts of sediment that it deposits in the sea. As a result, the river has created one of the world's largest deltas. About 50 small Inuit villages are located on the delta.

Winters in the Yukon are long and cold, with short periods of daylight. Much of this region freezes from October to June. In summer, when the river floods, millions of birds nest in the Yukon Delta National Wildlife Refuge.

The most famous area along the Yukon River is in Canada. In 1896, gold was discovered in some of the creeks that empty into the Klondike River, near where it joins with the Yukon. Thousands of people rushed to the area in the hope of becoming rich. At the fork where the two rivers meet, the town of Dawson was born. In just 2 years, its population grew to 16,000 people. Within a few years, however, gold production dropped and most people left the area.

Relatively few people live along the Yukon today, but the land surrounding the river is rich in wildlife. Grizzly bears, wolverines, lynx, marten, mink, and large herds of reindeer live there. The river is full of salmon and other fish.

At one time, the river was the main means of transportation in the Alaskan interior and the Yukon Territory. But today, the river is used mostly for local travel.

Name: From Inuit Eskimo words meaning "great river"
Location: Canada and Alaska
Length and rank (in U.S.): 1,265 miles; 7th longest
Source: Lakes in Yukon Territory and British Columbia, Canada
Flows into: Bering Sea
Major U.S. tributaries: Porcupine, Tanana, Koyukuk, and Innoko Rivers
Drainage area: 328,000 square miles
Major U.S. cities: none
Fun fact: A rare bird called the "bristle-thighed curlew" spends the summer on the Yukon Delta. Then it flies to the South Pacific, over 2,000 miles away, for the winter.

Opposite page:
The Yukon River floods every summer and covers the surrounding plain.

America's Top 10 Rivers are the longest in the country. Below is a list of other major rivers in the United States.

America's Major Rivers

State: Rivers

Alabama: Alabama, Chattahoochee, Mobile, Tennessee, Tombigbee

Alaska: Cooper, Koyukuk, Kuskokwin, Porcupine, Susitna, Tanana, Yukon

Arizona: Colorado, Gila, Little Colorado, Santa Cruz

Arkansas: Arkansas, Black, Buffalo, Mississippi, Red

California: American, Colorado, Eel, Klamath, Sacramento, San Joaquin, Trinity

Colorado: Arkansas, Colorado, North Platte, Rio Grande, South Platte

Connecticut: Connecticut, Housatonic, Naugatuck, Thames

Delaware: Christina, Delaware, Indian, Mispillion, Nanticoke

Florida: Apalachicola, Caloosahatchee, Kissimmee, St. Johns, St. Marys, Suwannee

Georgia: Altamaha, Chattahoochee, Flint, Ogeechee, Satilla, Savannah

Hawaii: None

Idaho: Bear, Boise, Clearwater, Couer d'Alene, Salmon, Snake

Illinois: Green, Illinois, Mississippi, Ohio, Wabash

Indiana: Eel, Mississinewa, Ohio, Patoka, Tippecanoe, Wabash

Iowa: Cedar, Des Moines, Iowa, Little Sioux, Mississippi, Missouri, Skunk, Wapsipinicon

Kansas: Arkansas, Kansas, Missouri, Neosho, Saline, Smoky Hill, Solomon, Verdigris

Kentucky: Green, Kentucky, Licking, Mississippi, Ohio, Tennessee

Louisiana: Calcasieu, Mississippi, Ouachita, Pearl, Red, Sabine

Maine: Androscoggin, Kennebec, Penobscot, St. Croix, St. John

Maryland: Monacacy, Pocomoke, Potomac, Youghiogheny

Massachusetts: Charles, Concord, Connecticut, Deerfield, Housatonic, Merrimack, Tauton

Michigan: Detroit, Grand, Menominee, Muskegon, St. Clair, St. Marys

Minnesota: Minnesota, Mississippi, Red River of the North, St. Croix, St. Louis

Mississippi: Big Black, Chickasawhay, Mississippi, Pearl, Tombigbee, Yazoo

Missouri: Current, Gasconade, Meramec, Mississippi, Missouri, Osage, Salt, St. Francis

Montana: Jefferson, Madison, Marias, Missouri, Musselshell, Powder, Tongue, Yellowstone

Nebraska: Big Blue, Elkhorn, Little Blue, Loup, Niobrara, Platte, Republican

Nevada: Carson, Colorado, Humboldt, Reese, Truckee

New Hampshire: Androscoggin, Connecticut, Merrimack, Piscataqua, Saco, Salmon Falls

New Jersey: Hackensack, Maurice, Passaic, Raritan

New Mexico: Canadian, Gila, Pecos, Rio Grande, San Juan

New York: Delaware, Genesee, Hudson, Mohawk, Niagara, St. Lawrence, Susquehanna

North Carolina: Cape Fear, Catawba, Neuse, Roanoke, Tar-Pamlico, Yadkin-Pee Dee

North Dakota: Cedar, James, Little Missouri, Missouri, Sheyenne, Souris

Ohio: Cuyahoga, Great Miami, Little Miami, Muskingum, Ohio, Sandusky, Scioto

Oklahoma: Arkansas, Canadian, Cimarron, Red, Verdigris

Oregon: Columbia, John Day, Rogue, Snake, Umpqua, Willamette

Pennsylvania: Allegheny, Delaware, Lehigh, Monongahela, Schuylkill, Susquehanna

Rhode Island: Blackstone, Pawtucket

South Carolina: Broad, Edisto, Lynches, Pee Dee, Santee, Savannah

South Dakota: Bad, Big Sioux, Cheyenne, James, Missouri, Moreau, Vermillion, White

Tennessee: Cumberland, Duck, Hatchie, Mississippi, Tennessee

Texas: Brazos, Canadian, Colorado, Pecos, Red, Rio Grande, Sabine, Trinity

Utah: Bear, Colorado, Green, Jordan, Provo, San Juan, Weber

Vermont: Lamoille, Missisquoi, West, White, Winooski

Virginia: Clinch, Dan, James, New, Potomac, Rappahannock, Roanoke, Shenandoah, York

Washington: Columbia, Skagit, Snake, Spokane, Yakima

West Virginia: Big Sandy, Guyandotte, Greenbrier, Kanawha, Monongahela, Ohio, Potomac

Wisconsin: Black, Chippewa, Fox, Mississippi, Rock, St. Croix, Wisconsin, Wolf

Wyoming: Belle Fourche, Bighorn, Cheyenne, Green, North Platte, Powder, Snake, Yellowstone

See page 233 for more information about rivers.

AMERICA'S TOP

10

SKYSCRAPERS

CANADA

VT   ME

NH

NY

MA

CT   R

PA

Chrysler
Building

MD   NJ

The Chrysler Building

When it was completed in 1930, the Chrysler Building, in New York City, was the tallest building in the world. A year later, this 1,046-foot skyscraper was surpassed in height by the nearby Empire State Building. Today, the Chrysler Building is seventh tallest in the United States. The building is not known for its height, however. It is famous for the decorative details extending from its lobby to its peak.

The many design elements in the Chrysler Building were inspired by American automobiles. The reason for this unusual theme is that the building was named after Walter P. Chrysler, the founder of the Chrysler Corporation, which has been manufacturing cars since 1925. The building's exterior is decorated with huge, stainless steel sculptures of automobiles, radiator caps, and eagles. Also on the outside, above the 26th floor, are cars made out of gray and white bricks with steel hubcaps. In the lobby, a mural painted on the ceiling shows scenes from the Chrysler Corporation's factories. The tower on top of the building is made of stainless steel. It is constructed of 6 arcs, one on top of the other.

When it was built, the Chrysler Building contained technical features never before used, such as a central vacuum cleaning system. Called "the city within a city," the building was a self-contained community. Inside were an astonishing number of services: barbershops and beauty parlors, 2 gyms, a restaurant, and even 2 hospital emergency rooms! The Chrysler Building was truly ahead of its time.

Location: New York, New York
Opened: April 1930
Materials: Steel and stone
Height: 1,046 feet
Number of stories: 77
Cost: $15 million
Fun fact: 391,831 rivets, or metal bolts, were used to build the Chrysler Building.

Opposite page:
When the Chrysler Building first opened, one writer described the 6 arcs at the top as 6 sunbursts.

CANADA

NY

VT
NH
ME
MA
CT
RI

PA

NJ

MD

Empire
State
Building

The
Empire State Building

In the 1933 movie *King Kong*, the Empire State Building in New York is featured in one of the most memorable scenes of motion picture history. In it, the giant Kong climbs to the very top of the 1,250-foot skyscraper. The Empire State Building had been built 2 years before the movie was made, and was then the world's tallest building. Today it ranks seventh tallest in the world and fourth tallest in the United States.

The Empire State Building was named one of the 7 civil engineering wonders of the world by the American Society of Civil Engineers. Its sleek design set a new standard for the construction of tall buildings. The building's main shaft soars upward, ending in a series of step-like indentations called "setbacks." The slender tower at the top points toward the sky like a giant, metal finger.

The Empire State Building has 102 floors. On the 86th floor is a famous observatory. The building's 73 elevators operate at speeds of 600 to 1,400 feet a minute. On top of the observatory is a transmission tower used by 3 New York City television stations and 17 FM radio stations.

The Empire State Building was so well engineered that its structural safety was not harmed when a U.S. Air Force B-25 bomber crashed into its 79th floor in 1945 on July 28. Only the interior of 2 floors were damaged by the accident.

What may be most remarkable about the Empire State Building is the speed with which this huge structure was built. The workers finished the job in only 1 year and 45 days.

Location: New York, New York
Opened: May 1931
Materials: Aluminum, granite, limestone, steel
Height: Building 1,250 feet; television tower 214 feet
Number of stories: 102
Cost: $40,948,900
Fun fact: The Empire State Building contains 60,000 tons of steel—enough to build a double-track railroad from New York City to Baltimore.

Opposite page:
The step-like setbacks near the top of the Empire State Building were a revolutionary design.

AMERICA'S TOP

10

SKYSCRAPERS

OR

ID

NV

UT

Pacific Ocean

CA

AZ

**First Interstate
World Center**

MEXICO

SHERATON
GRANDE

The First Interstate World Center

The First Interstate World Center in Los Angeles, California, is the tallest skyscraper west of Chicago. Since it was opened in 1990, the building has become the most recognized modern landmark in Los Angeles. It has a cylindrical shape that tapers from the base to the peak. Atop the white marble building is a circular glass crown that is illuminated at night. The crown is not simply a decoration. It houses the building's air-conditioning equipment. Above the lobby entrance is a dramatic mural made of metal with images that show scenes from the city's past.

Los Angeles residents often refer to the First Interstate World Center as Library Tower because it stands next to the old Los Angeles Central Library, a landmark that was built in the 1920s. Citizens worried that construction of the First Interstate World Center would require that the library be torn down. That did not happen. Instead, the developers of the new skyscraper worked to restore the old library and even replanted the library lawn, which had been paved over as a parking lot.

The First Interstate World Center was designed to enrich the neighborhood in which it was built. To the west of the north entrance and running alongside the building is a large public space called the Bunker Hill Steps. These spectacular steps were inspired by the Spanish Steps in Rome. They connect two business areas of the city that had been divided by a wall. The First Interstate World Center is proof that a skyscraper can also be a work of art.

Location: Los Angeles, California
Opened: January 1990
Materials: Concrete, marble, steel
Height: 1,108 feet
Number of stories: 73
Cost: $450 million
Fun fact: The Bunker Hill Steps cover a distance of 50 feet.

Opposite page:
The white marble exterior of the First Interstate World Center contrasts with the blue L.A. sky.

AMERICA'S TOP

10

SKYSCRAPERS

WI

IA

John
Hancock
Center

IL

MI

OH

IN

MO

KY

The John Hancock Center

The John Hancock Center, in Chicago, stands 1,127 feet high. Its twin 349-foot antennae are used by 8 television stations and 12 radio stations.

The big, black skyscraper is known best for its pioneering structural design. Most skyscrapers are supported by an interior skeleton of steel beams that braces the building against the wind. The outer walls merely hang on the skeleton like a curtain (they are called "curtain walls"). At the John Hancock Center, however, winds are offset by steel braces in the exterior walls. This type of construction uses less steel and increases the amount of interior space.

The outer "skin," or covering, of black aluminum contrasts with the John Hancock Center's many bronze windows, giving it a dramatic appearance. The structure's 1,250 miles of electrical wiring transmit enough power to supply a city of 30,000 people. The actual building takes up only 40 percent of the site on which it stands. The rest of the area is open space—rare in the heart of this city.

This building was constructed for the John Hancock Mutual Insurance Company. In the observatory on the top floor are a number of interesting displays, including a letter written by John Hancock, the first person to sign the Declaration of Independence. Since Chicago residents love their city's professional sports teams, they are also represented in the observatory. On display are a golden bull from the Chicago Bulls basketball team and baseballs autographed by the White Sox and the Cubs.

Location: Chicago, Illinois
Opened: March 1970
Materials: Aluminum, concrete, glass, steel
Height: Building 1,127 feet; antennae 349 feet
Number of stories: 100
Cost: $100 million
Fun fact: The frame of the building contains enough steel to make 33,000 cars.

Opposite page:
The John Hancock Center helped to pioneer a new kind of structural design.

AMERICA'S TOP

10

SKYSCRAPERS

TN

SC

★ **NationsBank Plaza**

AL

GA

FL

The NationsBank Plaza

During the 1980s and early 1990s, the skyline of Atlanta, Georgia, underwent striking changes. Skyscrapers began to rise with amazing speed, like mushrooms popping out of the ground after a rainstorm. The tallest of these buildings is the NationsBank Plaza, which was completed in February 1992. It was a massive construction job and was finished in a surprisingly short time. The 1,023-foot-high building required 24,000 tons of steel and 68,400 cubic yards of concrete. It took 17,000 truckloads to remove the earth that was excavated from the building site. Workers called the building schedule the "blast track"—even faster than the "fast track!" Only 2 years after construction began, the first tenants were moving into the building—a remarkable achievement. The architects worked closely with the contractor—the person who supervised the construction process—in order to complete the project quickly.

The NationsBank Plaza is supported by what architects call "super columns." Each column is made of a steel frame encased in concrete. All 8 of the super columns are located on the outside of the building. By placing the building's supporting structures entirely on the exterior, designers provided for more usable space inside. The outside of the building is an aluminum framework that holds red granite and bronze-tinted windows. Atop the roof is a steel cage that resembles a pyramid with steps. At night, the cage is illuminated and can be seen for miles.

Location: Atlanta, Georgia
Opened: February 1992
Materials: Concrete, granite, steel
Height: 1,023 feet
Number of stories: 55
Cost: $117 million
Fun fact: The construction schedule called for 4 days of work per floor. It was shortened to 3 per floor.

Opposite page:
The NationsBank building was designed to have 8 supporting columns on its exterior.

AMERICA'S TOP

10

SKYSCRAPERS

CANADA
NY
PA
One
Liberty
Place
NJ
OH
WV
MD
VA
DE

One Liberty Place

In 1986, on September 10, William Penn's 3-cornered hat was no longer the highest point in Philadelphia, Pennsylvania. Until that day, it was a custom in Philadelphia that no building should be taller than the statue of William Penn, which stands atop City Hall. (Penn was the Colonial leader who founded Philadelphia.) The tradition was broken, however, when a construction-crane operator lifted the first of several steel columns used to frame the 44th floor of One Liberty Place. When One Liberty Place was completed, the 959-foot building was almost double the height of "Billy Penn's" statue.

One Liberty Place is not only taller than any building in Philadelphia—it has a different shape. Most tall buildings in the city have flat tops. One Liberty Place is crowned by a glass pyramid, topped by a spire.

Like NationsBank Plaza, One Liberty Place is supported by a dozen "super columns." Four of these columns form a rectangular core in the center of the building. The other columns are on the outside of the building, 2 of them on each of the 4 walls. The exterior of One Liberty Place is covered by granite and glass. The base is completely clad in granite. As the building increases in height, more glass is used in place of granite. Finally, at the top, the building is all glass. The architects felt that this transition from stone to glass mirrored the change in landscape from earth to sky.

Location: Philadelphia, Pennsylvania
Opened: February 1988
Materials: Concrete, glass, granite, steel
Height: 945 feet
Number of stories: 61
Cost: $200 million
Fun fact: One Liberty Place has 28 elevators.

Opposite page:
The graceful pyramid and spire atop One Liberty Place contrast with the surrounding flat-topped buildings.

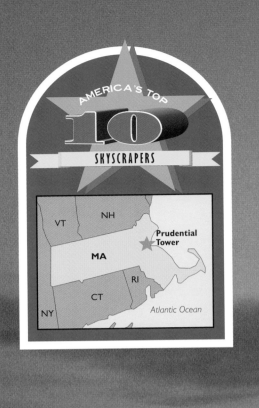

AMERICA'S TOP

10

SKYSCRAPERS

VT
NH
MA
Prudential
Tower
RI
CT
NY
Atlantic Ocean

The Prudential Tower

★ ★ ★ ★ ★ ★ ★   ★ ★ ★ ★ ★ ★ ★

The Prudential Tower, in Boston, Massachusetts, crowns an indoor shopping mall. The mall is surrounded by an outdoor plaza. Together, the plaza, mall, and tower are referred to as the Prudential Center. Standing 750 feet high, not including its television mast, the tower has a total of 10 acres, or 435,600 square feet of glass—a large amount for a building of its size. Two million fasteners were required to seal the 10,000 windows in place. Although it is not the tallest building in Boston—the John Hancock Center is 38 feet higher—Prudential Tower is recognized by most Bostonians as the most significant structure in the city. They often refer to it as the "Pru."

The Prudential Center and its tower were built over the Conrail railroad tracks and the Massachusetts Turnpike—a major road that crosses much of the state. To allow the tracks and highway to run beneath the site, the center was raised 18 feet above street level. The center's parking garage was split into two sections by the tracks and turnpike.

The tower itself, topped by 13-foot-high letters that spell "Prudential," is visible far beyond the city limits. The walls of this rectangular building are 150 by 178 feet wide. The structural steel that forms the internal skeleton of the tower weighs 60 million pounds. The building's foundations reach 170 feet below the ground.

Today, the Prudential Tower is considered to be as much a Boston landmark as Fenway Park, home of the Red Sox baseball team.

Location: Boston, Massachusetts
Opened: September 8, 1964
Materials: Concrete and steel
Height: 750 feet
Number of stories: 52
Cost: $200 million
Fun fact: The elevators take only 30 seconds to reach the observation deck on the 50th floor.

Opposite page:
The Prudential Tower is reflected on the Charles River.

AMERICA'S TOP

10

SKYSCRAPERS

Sears
Tower

WI

IA

MO

IL

MI

OH

IN

KY

Harrison
HOTEL
PARK FREE

TORCO

The Sears Tower

★ ★ ★ ★ ★ ★ ★ ★ ★ ★ ★ ★ ★ ★ ★

Until the middle of the 1990s, the Sears Tower, in Chicago, was recognized as the world's tallest building. Then construction of the Petronas Twin Towers in Malaysia changed the rank of the Sears Tower to Number 2, according to the Council on Tall Buildings and Urban Habitat.

The tower, at 1,454 feet high, is nevertheless one of the most impressive structures ever built. Everything about it is big. In a city of massive buildings, it stands well above the others. The Sears Tower has 110 stories with 4.5 million feet of floor space, the equivalent of 101 acres! The tower has 16,100 bronze-tinted windows, which are washed by 6 machines mounted on the roof. The bronzed windows contrast with the tower's outer wall of black aluminum, giving the building a spectacular exterior. The tower contains 76,000 tons of structural steel—enough to build more than 52,000 automobiles. The 104 elevators in the building operate at a speed of up to 1,600 feet a minute. They are among the fastest in the world.

The tower was originally built to house the headquarters of Sears, Roebuck and Co. Its design was completed in July 1970 and construction began a month later. By September 1973, the first Sears employees began moving into the building. Nine years later, the antennae atop the structure were completed. They are used by more than 20 radio and TV stations. After Sears moved its headquarters to the Chicago suburbs in 1993, the tower was renovated to accommodate many other companies and organizations.

Location: Chicago, Illinois
Opened: 1973
Materials: Aluminum, concrete, glass, steel
Height: 1,454 feet, antennae 253 feet
Number of stories: 110
Cost: Over $150 million
Fun fact: The Sears Tower has 25,000 miles of plumbing pipe and 2,000 miles of electrical wire.

Opposite page:
The tall antennae of the Sears Tower seem to pierce the sky.

AMERICA'S TOP

10

SKYSCRAPERS

Transamerica
Pyramid

Pacific Ocean

OR

ID

NV

UT

CA

AZ

MEXICO

The Transamerica Pyramid

The Transamerica Pyramid, in San Francisco, is one of the most striking skyscrapers in the world. It is a slender structure that is shaped like a pyramid with a pair of windowless wings rising up from the 29th floor. Although some of the city's residents did not like the building at first, it has become a landmark that is admired by San Francisco's visitors and residents alike.

The designers of the pyramid patterned the building after the famous redwood trees of northern California. Like the tall redwoods, the building tapers as its height increases. This design allows more light to reach the streets than the design of rectangular skyscrapers. Once the pyramid was opened, it became a popular place to visit. Next door is the Transamerica Redwood Park, a half-acre site on which redwoods have been planted.

The pyramid is also noted for its many safety features. In particular, it was built to withstand strong earthquakes. While skyscrapers usually rest on pilings sunk into the earth, the pyramid stands on a slab of concrete 9 feet thick. Automatic water sprinklers for fighting fires were installed on each floor, and in the building's west wing, there is a shaft that allows smoke to escape. The other wing contains an elevator shaft that serves the higher floors.

Since it was opened, the pyramid has been featured on postcards, in movies, and on television. It has become one of the best-known landmarks of San Francisco.

Location: San Francisco, California
Opened: August 1972
Materials: Concrete and steel
Height: 853 feet
Number of stories: 48
Cost: $43 million
Fun fact: The Transamerica Pyramid has 3,678 windows.

Opposite page:
The unusual design of the Transamerica Pyramid was inspired by redwood trees.

AMERICA'S TOP

10

SKYSCRAPERS

CANADA

ME

VT

NH

NY

MA

RI

CT

PA

NJ

World Trade Center

MD

The World Trade Towers

The World Trade Center, in New York City, is a complex of 7 buildings, including the famed twin towers—the second- and third-tallest buildings in America. The tower at One World Trade Center rises 1,368 feet—6 feet higher than its twin. Each tower is so large that it has its own individual postal ZIP code!

This huge building complex was commissioned, or ordered, by the Port Authority of New York and New Jersey, the transportation agency for the two states. Excavation of the site, which began in 1966, took 2 years. More than 1.2 million cubic yards of earth and rock had to be removed before the buildings' steel frames could be constructed. The base of each center weighed 1.3 million tons, and required 425,000 cubic yards of concrete—enough to build a sidewalk from New York City to Washington, D.C.

The design of the twin towers included a pioneering advance in skyscraper construction that was also used in Chicago's John Hancock Center. Up to that point, the typical skyscraper of the period had an internal skeleton of steel columns. This skeleton supported the weight and braced against the wind. Most of the steel in the twin towers, however, is on the outside, which increases the amount of usable space within.

In 1993, on February 26, a terrorist bomb exploded at the World Trade Center. It killed 6 people and injured more than 1,000. Both towers were extensively damaged, but repairs were made quickly, and they were reopened a month later.

Location: New York, New York
Opened: December 1970
Materials: Concrete and steel
Height: Tower One 1,368 feet; television mast 360 feet; Tower Two 1,362 feet
Number of stories: 110 in each tower
Cost: $800 million
Fun fact: The Top of the World observation deck in Tower Two draws 1.8 million visitors per year.

Opposite page:
The twin towers of the World Trade Center soar above the older buildings of lower Manhattan.

America's Top 10 Skyscrapers are not necessarily the highest. Although height was one basis for including a building in this volume, we also considered a skyscraper's cultural and architectural significance. Below is a list of some other notable skyscrapers.

More American Skyscrapers		
Building	**Height**	**Location**
American International Building	950 feet	New York, New York
Amoco Building	1,136 feet	Chicago, Illinois
Citicorp Center	915 feet	New York, New York
Columbia Seafirst Center	943 feet	Seattle, Washington
First Interstate Bank Plaza	972 feet	Houston, Texas
40 Wall Street	927 feet	New York, New York
John Hancock Center	788 feet	Boston, Massachusetts
Texas Commerce Tower	1,000 feet	Houston, Texas
311 South Wacker Drive	959 feet	Chicago, Illinois
Transco Tower	901 feet	Houston, Texas
Two Prudential Plaza	978 feet	Chicago, Illinois

Houston Skyline

See page 233 for more information about skyscrapers.

GLOSSARY

abutments Supports, usually made of concrete, at either end of a bridge.

aerospace The study and industry of flight/aviation.

agriculture The business of raising crops and livestock; farming.

altitude The vertical height or elevation of an object above the earth's surface.

anchor bolt A large bolt used to attach a structure to its foundation.

annual ring The annual growth of a tree.

approach A roadway or trestle leading to a bridge.

archaeologist A person trained to study the way people of ancient cultures lived.

architect A person trained to design buildings and other structures.

asteroid One of the many small, solid objects made of rock or metal that orbits the Sun.

bank The land along the edge of a river or other body of water.

bedrock The solid rock that is found beneath the surface of the earth.

bluff A steep river bank.

burl A hard, woody rounded outgrowth on a tree.

cable Very strong rope made of wire.

calving Here, the process by which icebergs are formed when chunks of ice break off a larger ice wall and fall into the ocean.

canal A human-made waterway.

cantilever bridge A bridge that has 2 sections— each one anchored to the shore. The sections extend over the water but don't meet. They are joined by a third section—the center span.

canyon A narrow passage with steep rocky sides, formed by a river.

centennial Occurring once every 100 years.

channel The deep part of a river or harbor.

cirque A bowl-shaped valley.

clad Completely covered.

clearance The space between the surface of the water and the span of the bridge.

Colonial days The time before the American Revolution, when America was a British colony.

colony A group of similar organisms that live in a particular area.

conveyor A mechanical device for moving bulk material from place to place.

cornerstone The first stone laid in the foundation of a structure.

crater A bowl-shaped hole in the ground formed by a meteorite, volcano, or geyser.

creeper derrick A piece of construction equipment that has a platform, crane, and a set of tracks. It is designed to climb the structure being built.

crust The outer layer of the earth.

dam A barrier built across a river. Dams are built to control the flow of water or to raise the water level.

deciduous trees Trees that shed their leaves in autumn.

dedicated Opened to the public.

delta A deposit of soil and other sediment at the mouth of a river.

deposit Matter that settles out of water—for example, when water evaporates.

drainage area The land that contributes water to a river and all its tributaries.

dredge Deepen, widen, or clean a body of water using a machine called a dredge.

duct A tube, pipe, or channel.

earthquake A sudden shaking of the earth's crust.

elevation Distance above sea level.

echolocation The ability to use reflected sounds for navigation.

engineer A person who designs buildings or large public works, such as bridges, dams, and canals.

erode To wear away slowly by the action of water, wind, or glacial ice.

erosion The wearing away of land by rain, wind, glacial action, or running water.

ethnic A national, racial, religious, or cultural group—for example, Chinese-Americans.

evaporate Change from a liquid to a gaseous state.

evergreen trees Trees that have leaves year-round.

excavation The process of removing by digging.

fault A crack or break in the earth's crust along which movement occurs.

fossil The remains, impression, or trace of an animal or plant from past ages that have been preserved in the earth's crust.

foundation The underlying part of a structure that supports its upper part.

freeway A high-speed road with several lanes and no intersections or stoplights.

geyser A hot spring that periodically shoots water and steam into the air.

glacier A large body of ice that moves slowly over land or down a mountain slope.

granite A hard rock made of quartz and other minerals.

gravity The force of attraction that pulls objects toward the center of the earth.

Ice Age A prehistoric time period when glaciers covered much of the earth's surface.

illuminated Brightened with light.

immigrant A person who comes to a country to settle there permanently.

inaugural Marking the beginning.

inscribe To write, carve, or engrave words or symbols on something.

kivas Chambers used by Native American men for ceremonial purposes.

lava Molten rock.

levee A mound built along a river bank to prevent the river from overflowing.

liberty Freedom.

limestone A type of soft rock formed mostly from the accumulated remains of living things, such as seashells.

lock A section of a river closed off with gates. Boats can be raised or lowered by raising or lowering the water level in the lock.

magma Molten, or hot, liquid rock material within the earth.

main span The stretch of bridge between the towers.

meander To follow a turning or winding course.

meteor A mass of stone or metal from outer space that reaches Earth.

migrate To move seasonally from one region to another.

mission A church building or community used to help spread Christianity.

model A copy of something, usually built on a smaller scale.

mouth The place where a river empties into a larger body of water.

navigable Deep enough and wide enough for boat travel.

notch A deep, narrow pass through a mountain range.

obelisk A tall, tapering structure first built by ancient Egyptians.

pedestal An architectural support or base, as for a column or statue.

permafrost A permanently frozen layer below the earth's surface.

pier A support under a bridge usually made of steel or concrete.

pilings Long columns of steel, wood, or concrete that are driven into the ground to support the weight of a heavy structure.

pipeline A line of welded pipe with valves and pumps that is used to transport liquids or gases.

plateau An area of flat land that is raised above the surrounding area.

plume A shape like a long feather.

pontoon A floating structure that supports a floating bridge.

prehistoric The period before recorded history.

pyramid A structure or object used in ancient Egypt that has a square base and 4 triangular walls that meet in a point at the top.

range A group of mountains.

rapids The place where a riverbed descends steeply, causing the water to move fast.

reservoir An artificial lake created by a dam.

restore To bring back to its original state.

river system All the streams and rivers that empty their water—directly or indirectly—into a major river.

sculptor One who shapes or molds material into an artistic form.

sea level The average level of the surface of the world's oceans. Sea level is the starting point for measuring the elevation of mountains.

sediment Particles of soil and other materials carried by flowing water and eventually deposited.

shaft In this book, part of a structure shaped like a long column.

skeleton A supporting framework or structure.

skyscraper A very tall building.

source The place where a river begins.

span The spread of the bridge between the abutments.

spillway A channel that allows excess water to run over or around an obstruction.

stalactite The deposit of a mineral substance on the roof or side of a cave or cavern that resembles an icicle.

stalagmite A formation that looks like a cone projecting from the floor of a cave.

stockyard A large, enclosed area where cattle or other animals are kept until they are slaughtered or shipped to other areas.

structural steel Steel designed for building the framework of bridges and buildings.

summit The top of a mountain.

suspension bridge A bridge with a roadway that hangs by steel "suspenders" from steel cables, which are in turn held up by 2 towers.

temperate A climate that is mild—neither hot (tropical) nor cold (arctic).

theory A possible—but unproven—answer to a question.

tidal pool A small body of water filled by the ocean twice a day during high tide.

time capsule A sealed container included in a structure, or buried by itself, that contains items of the time. The capsule is intended to be opened in the distant future.

trading post A store in an area with few people, where goods are often traded rather than sold. For example, a trader may exchange clothing or blankets for a bushel of corn.

tree line The area on a mountain above which trees rarely grow.

trestle A braced frame used to support a bridge.

tributary A river that flows into a larger one.

tundra An area above the tree line on mountains and in arctic regions, where the soil beneath the top layer is permanently frozen.

FOR MORE INFORMATION

Bridges

BOOKS

Ardley, Neil. *Bridges*. Ada, OK: Garrett Educational Corporation, 1990.

Doherty, Craig, and Katherine Doherty. *The Golden Gate Bridge*. Woodbridge, CT: Blackbirch Press, 1995.

Pascoe, Elaine. *The Brooklyn Bridge* (Building America). Woodbridge, CT: Blackbirch Press, 1999.

Pelta, Kathy. *Bridging the Golden Gate*. Minneapolis: Lerner Publications Co., 1987.

Robbins, Ken. *Bridges*. New York: Dial Books, 1991.

Spagenburg, Ray, and Diane Moser. *The Story of America's Bridges*. New York: Facts On File, 1991.

WEB SITES

Brooklyn Bridge http://romdog.com/bridge/brooklyn.html

Golden Gate Bridge http://www.goldengate.org

San Francisco–Oakland Bay Bridge http://www.sfmuseum.org/hist2/bbridge.html

Verrazano–Narrows Bridge http://www.mta.nyc.ny.us/bandt/html/veraz.htm

Cities

BOOKS

Aylesworth, Thomas and Virginia Aylesworth *Chicago: Hub of the Midwest*. Woodbridge, CT: Blackbirch Press, 1990.

Balcer, Bernadete and Fran O'Bryne-Pelham. *Philadelphia*. Morristown, NJ: Silver Burdett, 1988.

Bredeson, Carmen. *The Battle of the Alamo: The Fight for Texas Territory*. Brookfield, CT: Millbrook Press, 1996.

Doherty, Craig A. and Katherine M. Doherty. *The Houston Astrodome*. Woodbridge, CT: Blackbirch Press, 1996.

———. *The Sears Tower*. Woodbridge, CT: Blackbirch Press, 1995.

———. *The Statue of Liberty*. Woodbridge, CT: Blackbirch Press, 1996.

Fein, Art. *L.A. Musical Tour: A Guide to the Rock and Roll Landmarks of Los Angeles*. Winchester, MA: Faber and Faber, 1991.

Glassman, Bruce. *New York: Gateway to the New World*. Woodbridge, CT: Blackbirch Press, 1991.

Lee, Sally. *San Antonio*. Morristown, NJ: Silver Burdett, 1992.

Luhrs, Ruth J. *Kidding Around San Diego: A Young Person's Guide to the City*. Santa Fe, NM: John Muir Publications, 1991.

Moeser, June. *Four Sentinels: The Story of San Diego's Lighthouses.* San Diego, CA: Tecolote Press, 1991.

Riley, Edward M. *Starting America: The Story of Independence Hall.* Gettysburg, PA: Thomas Publications, 1990.

Stewart, G. *Houston.* Vero Beach, FL: Rourke, 1989.

————. *Los Angeles.* Vero Beach, FL: Rourke, 1989.

Zelver, Patricia. *The Wonderful Towers of Watts.* New York: Morrow, 1994.

Zimmerman, Chanda K. *Detroit.* Morristown, NJ: Silver Burdett, 1989.

WEB SITES

Chicago http://www.ci.chi.il.us

Dallas http://www.ci.dallas.tx.us

Detroit http://www.ci.detroit.mi.us

Houston http://www.ci.houston.tx.us

Los Angeles http://www.cityofla.org

New York http://www.ci.nyc.ny.us

Philadelphia http://www.phila.gov

Phoenix http://www.ci.phoenix.az.us

San Antonio http://www.ci.sat.tx.us

San Diego http://www.sannet.gov

Construction Wonders

BOOKS

Aylesworth, Thomas and Virginia. *Chicago.* Woodbridge, CT: Blackbirch Press, 1990.

Boring, Mel. *Incredible Constructions and the People Who Built Them.* New York: Walker & Co., 1985.

Doherty, Craig and Katherine Doherty. *Building America: The Sears Tower.* Woodbridge, CT: Blackbirch Press, 1995.

————. *Building America: The Gateway Arch.* Woodbridge, CT: Blackbirch Press, 1995.

————. *Building America: The Seattle Space Needle.* Woodbridge, CT: Blackbirch Press, 1995.

————. *Building America: The Erie Canal.* Woodbridge, CT: Blackbirch Press, 1997.

Duncan, Michael. *How Skyscrapers Are Made.* New York: Facts On File, 1987.

Nirgiotis, Nicholas. *Erie Canal: Gateway to the West.* New York: Franklin Watts, 1993.

Ricciuti, Edward. *America's Top 10 Skyscrapers.* Woodbridge, CT: Blackbirch Press, 1997.

————. *America's Top 10 Bridges.* Woodbridge, CT: Blackbirch Press, 1997.

Stone, Tanya Lee. *America's Top 10 National Monuments.* Woodbridge, CT: Blackbirch Press, 1997.

Stein, R. Conrad. *The Story of the Erie Canal.* Chicago: Childrens Press, 1985.

WEB SITES

Alaska Pipeline http://www.alyeska-pipe.com

Disney World's Epcot Center http://www.disney.go.com/disneyworld/themeparks

Gateway Arch http://www.nps.gov/jeff/arch-home

Hubble Space Telescope http://www.stsci.edu

Lincoln Tunnel http://www.panynj.gov

Louisiana Superdome http://www.superdome.com

Seattle Space Needle http://www.spaceneedle.com

Curiosities

BOOKS

Bolt, Bruce A. *Discover Volcanoes and Earthquakes*. Lake Forest, IL: Forest House, 1992.

Brewer, Duncan. *Comets, Asteroids and Meteorites*. Tarrytown, NY: Marshall Cavendish, 1992.

Butler, Daphne. *What Happens When Volcanoes Erupt?* Chatham, NJ: Raintree Steck-Vaughn, 1995.

Carlisle, Madelyn. *Let's Investigate Magical, Mysterious Meteorites*. Hauppauge, NY: Barron's Educational Series, 1992.

Lauber, Patricia. *Voyagers from Space: Meteors and Meteorites*. New York: HarperCollins Children's Books, 1989.

WEB SITES

To learn more about the fascinating world of bats, visit the web site for Bat Conservation International, Inc., at http://www.batcon.org

Visit the **Bristlecone Pines** website at http://www.sonic.net/bristlecone/intro.html

Visit **Meteor Crater** Enterprises, Inc., at http://www.meteorcrater.com

To view some of the unusual phenomena at the **Mystery Spot**, visit their web page at http://www.mystery-spot.com

For a closer look at Hawaii's volcanoes, visit Hawaii Volcanoes National Park at http://www.book.uci.edu/Books/Moon/volcanoes.html

To learn more about **Yellowstone National Park**, visit the park's web site at http://www.nps.gov/yell

Mountains

BOOKS

Arvetis, Chris and Carole Palmer. *Mountains*. Skokie, IL: Rand McNalley & Co., 1993.

Barnes-Svarney, Patricia L. *Born of Heat and Pressure: Mountains and Metamorphic Rocks*. Springfield, NJ: Enslow, 1991.

Bradley, Catherine. *Life in the Mountains*. New York: Scholastic, Inc., 1993.

Bramwell, Martyn. *Mountains*. New York: Franklin Watts, 1994.

Collinson, Allan. *Mountains*. Morristown, NJ: Silver Burdett, 1992.

Knapp, Brian. *Volcano*. Chatham, NJ: Raintree Steck-Vaughn, 1990.

Lauber, Patricia. *Volcanoes and Earthquakes*. New York: Scholastic, Inc., 1991.

Mariner, Tom. *Mountains*. Tarrytown, NY: Marshall Cavendish, 1990.

Steele, Philip. *Mountains*. Morristown, NJ: Silver Burdett, 1991.

Tilling, Robert I. *Born of Fire: Volcanoes and Igneous Rocks*. Springfield, NJ: Enslow, 1991.

WEB SITES

Grand Teton http://www.nps.gov/grte

Mauna Kea http://www.book.uci.edu/Books/Moon/mauna_kea.html

Mount McKinley http://www.nps.gov/dena

Mount Rainier http://www.ohwy.com/wa/m/mtrainnp.htm

Mount Saint Elias http://www.nps.gov/wrst

Mount Washington http://www.whitemtn.org/wma99/1999/mtwash.html

Mount Whitney http://www.nps.gov/seki/whitney.htm

National Monuments

BOOKS

Ayer, Eleanor. *I Know America: Our National Monuments*. Brookfield, CT: The Millbrook Press, 1992.

Brown, Richard, illus. *A Kid's Guide to Washington, D.C.* New York: Harcourt Brace Jovanovich, 1989.

Coerr Eleanor. *Lady With a Torch: How the Statue of Liberty Was Born*. New York: Harper and Row, 1986.

Doherty, Craig and Katherine Doherty. *Building America: Mount Rushmore*. Woodbridge, CT: Blackbirch Press, 1995.

———. *Building America: The Statue of Liberty*. Woodbridge, CT: Blackbirch Press, 1997.

———. *Building America: The Washington Monument*. Woodbridge, CT: Blackbirch Press, 1995.

Glassman, Bruce. *New York*. Woodbridge, CT: Blackbirch Press, 1991.

Kent, Deborah. *America the Beautiful: Colorado*. Chicago: Childrens Press, 1989.

———. *America the Beautiful: Washington, D.C.* Chicago: Childrens Press, 1991.

Shapiro, M.J. *How They Built the Statue of Liberty*. New York: Random House, 1994.

WEB SITES

The Cabrillo National Monument http://www.nps.gov/cabr/home.html

The George Washington Carver National Monument http://www.coax.net/people/LWF/carver.htm

The Jefferson Memorial http://www.nps.gov/thje

The Lincoln Memorial http://www.nps.gov/linc

Mesa Verde National Park http://www.nps.gov/meve

Mount Rushmore http://www.state.sd.us/state/executive/tourism/rushmore/rushmore.htm

The Statue of Liberty http://www.fieldtrip.com/ny/23637620.htm

The Vietnam Veterans Memorial http://www.nps.gov/vive

The Washington Monument http://www.nps.gov/wamo

The White House http://www.whitehouse.gov

National Parks

BOOKS

Abbeville Press Staff, *Ansel Adam's National Parks*. New York: Abbeville Press, 1994.

Bangley, Jane, editor. *The Complete Guide to America's National Parks*. New York: Fodor's Travel Publications, 1996.

Brown, Richard. *A Kid's Guide to National Parks*. Orlando, FL: Harcourt Brace, 1989.

Butcher, Devereux. *Exploring Our National Parks and Monuments*. Boulder, CO: Roberts Rinehart, 1995.

Crump, Donald J., editor. *Adventures in Your National Parks*. Washington, DC: The National Geographic Society, 1989.

Lovett, Sarah. *Kidding Around the National Parks of the Southwest: A Young Person's Guide*. Santa Fe, NM: John Muir Publications, 1990.

National Geographic's Guide to the National Parks of the United States. Washington, DC: The National Geographic Society, 1992.

Weber, Michael. *Our National Parks*. Brookfield, CT: Millbrook Press, 1994.

WEB SITES

Acadia National Park http://www.nps.gov/acad
Grand Canyon National Park http://www.nps.gov/grca
Grand Teton National Park http://www.nps.gov/grte
Great Smoky Mountains National Park http://www.nps.gov/grsm
Mammoth Cave National Park http://www.nps.gov/maca
Olympic National Park http://www.nps.gov/olym
Rocky Mountains National Park http://www.nps.gov/romo
Yellowstone National Park http://www.nps.gov/yell
Yosemite National Park http://www.nps.gov/yose
Zion National Park http://www.nps.gov/zion

Natural Wonders

BOOKS

Bryan, T. Scott. *Geysers: What They Are and How They Work.* Boulder, CO: Rinehart, Roberts Publishers, Inc., 1990.

Cork, Barbara and R. Morris. *Mysteries and Marvels of Nature.* Tulsa, OK: EDC Publishing, 1983.

Frahm, Randy. *Canyons.* Mankato, MN: Creative Education, 1994.

Goodman, Billy. *Natural Wonders and Disasters.* New York: Little, Brown and Co., 1991.

Markert, Jenny. *Glaciers and Icebergs.* Mankato, MN: Child's World, Inc., 1993.

Pearce, Q. L. *Quicksand and Other Earthly Wonders.* Morristown, NJ: Simon and Schuster, 1989.

Rigby, Susan. *Caves.* Mahwah, NJ: Troll Communications, LLC, 1993.

Vogt, Gregory L. *The Search for the Killer Asteroid.* Brookfield, CT: Millbrook Press, Inc., 1994.

Wonders of Nature Take-Along Library, 5 vols. New York: Random House, Inc., 1991.

WEB SITES

Devils Tower http://www.state.sd.us/tourism/devtower
Giant Redwoods http://www.nps.gov/redw
Glacier Bay http://www.nps.gov/glba
Grand Canyon http://www.thecanyon.com/nps/index.htm
Mammoth Cave http://www.nps.gov/maca
Meteor Crater http://www.meteorcrater.com
Niagara Falls http://www.nfcvb.com
Old Faithful http://www.nps.gov/yell
Rainbow Bridge http://www.infowest.com/Utah/canyonlands/rainbow.html
White Sands http://www.nps.gov/whsa

Rivers

BOOKS

Ayer, Eleanor. *Our Great Rivers and Waterways*. Brookfield, CT: Millbrook Press, 1994.

Bailey, Donna. *Rivers*. Austin, TX: Raintree Steck-Vaughn, 1990.

Clifford, Nick. *Incredible Earth*. New York: Dorling Kindersley, 1996.

Cooper, Jason. *The Mississippi Delta*. Vero Beach, FL: Rourke, 1995.

Louri, Peter. *In the Path of Lewis & Clark: Traveling the Missouri*. Parsippany, NJ: Silver Burdett, 1996.

Mariner, Tom. *Rivers*. Tarrytown, NY: Marshall Cavendish, 1990.

Morgan, Nina. *The Mississippi*. Austin, TX: Raintree Steck-Vaughn, 1993.

Palmer, Tim. *The Wind and Scenic Rivers of America*. Fort Myers Beach, FL: Island Press, 1993.

WEB SITES

The Colorado River http://river.ihs.gov

The Mississippi River http://www.greatriver.com

The Missouri River http://www.oldmanriver.com

The Yukon River http://cesdis.gsfc.nasa.gov/people/becker/yukon.html

Skyscrapers

BOOKS

Conlin, Stephen. *Fold-out Skyscrapers*. Skokie, IL: Rand McNally, 1995.

Doherty, Craig and Katherine Doherty. *Building America: The Sears Tower*. Woodbridge, CT: Blackbirch Press, 1995.

————. *Building America: The Empire State Building*. Woodbridge, CT: Blackbirch Press, 1998.

Duncan, Michael. *How Skyscrapers Are Made*. New York: Facts On File, 1987.

Dunn, Andrew. *Skyscrapers*. New York: Thomson Learning, 1993.

Gibbons, Gail. *Up Goes the Skyscraper!* New York: Simon and Schuster Children, 1986.

WEB SITES

Empire State Building http://www.esbnyc.com

One Liberty Place http://www.gim.net/libertyplace

Sears Tower http://www.sears-tower.com

Transamerica Pyramid http://www.cityinsights.com/sftransa.htm

World Trade Center http://www.wtca.org

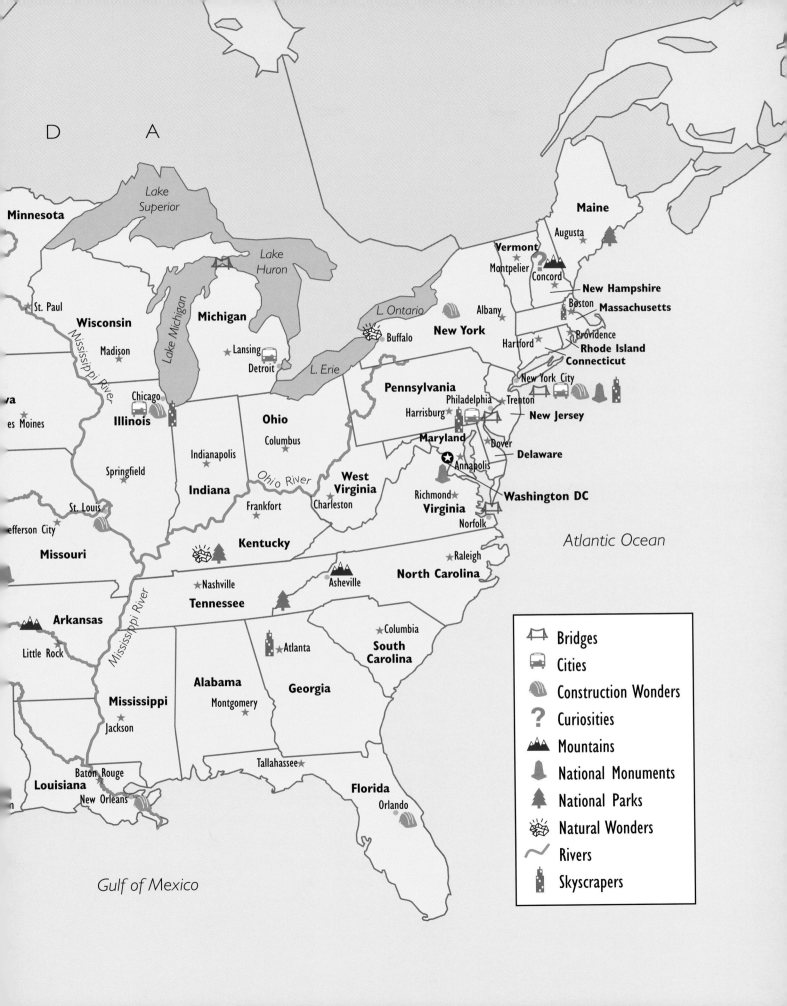

D A

Minnesota

Lake Superior

St. Paul

Wisconsin

Madison

Mississippi River

es Moines

Lake Michigan

Michigan

Lansing

Detroit

Lake Huron

L. Erie

Chicago

Illinois

Ohio

Columbus

Indianapolis

Springfield

Indiana

Ohio River

Frankfort

St. Louis

efferson City

Missouri

Mississippi River

Kentucky

Nashville

Tennessee

Arkansas

Little Rock

Alabama

Montgomery

Mississippi

Jackson

Baton Rouge

Louisiana

New Orleans

Tallahassee

Georgia

West Virginia

Charleston

Maine

Augusta

Vermont

Montpelier

Concord

New Hampshire

Boston

Massachusetts

Albany

New York

Hartford

Providence

Rhode Island

Connecticut

Buffalo

L. Ontario

Pennsylvania

Philadelphia

Trenton

New York City

Harrisburg

New Jersey

Maryland

Dover

Delaware

Annapolis

Washington DC

Richmond

Virginia

Norfolk

Raleigh

North Carolina

Asheville

Columbia

Atlanta

South Carolina

Florida

Orlando

Atlantic Ocean

Gulf of Mexico

	Bridges
	Cities
	Construction Wonders
?	Curiosities
	Mountains
	National Monuments
	National Parks
	Natural Wonders
	Rivers
	Skyscrapers

INDEX

Photo Credits

Page 6: ©Bruce Glassman/Blackbirch Press, Inc.; page 8: Courtesy of the Chesapeake Bay Bridge and Tunnel District; page 10: Courtesy of the Oregon Tourism Commission; page 12: Courtesy of the Washington State Department of Transportation; page 14: ©Jim McWilliams/Jim McWilliams Photography; page 16: ©Robert Holmes/California Division of Tourism; page 18: Courtesy of the Michigan Travel Bureau; page 20: Courtesy of Royal Gorge Bridge; pages 22, 220: ©Kerrick James/San Francisco Convention and Visitors Bureau; page 24: MTA Bridges and Tunnels photo; pages 26, 28, 34, 40, 44, 92, 106, 124, 136, 160, 172, 174, 180, 198, 224: PhotoDisc, Inc.; page 30: Courtesy of the Dallas Convention and Visitors Bureau; page 32: Vito Palmisano/ Courtesy of the Michigan Travel Bureau; pages 36, 208: Courtesy of the Los Angeles Convention and Visitors Bureau/©1991 Michele and Tom Grimm; pages 38, 122, 128, 130, 132, 134, 204, 206, 222: ©Blackbirch Press, Inc.; page 42: ©John Clare du Bois/Photo Researchers, Inc.; page 46: ©George Schaub/Leo de Wys, Inc.; page 50: Courtesy of Alyeska Pipeline Service Company; page 52: ©Steve Vidler/Leo de Wys, Inc.; page 54: New York State Thruway Authority; page 56: Courtesy of the St. Louis Convention and Visitors Commission; page 58: United States Department of the Interior/Bureau of Reclamation; page 60: Courtesy of NASA; page 62: Port Authority of New York and New Jersey; page 64: Louisiana Office of Tourism; page 66: ©Joseph Nettis/Photo Researchers, Inc.; page 68: Courtesy of Space Needle Corporation; page 70: Corel Corporation; page 72: Merlin D. Tuttle, Bat Conservation International; page 74: ©Robert Holmes/California Division of Tourism; pages 76, 126, 190: Photo by South Dakota Tourism; page 78: Photo by Kirby Warnoch ©Trans Pecos Productions; pages 80, 170: Meteor Crater, Northern Arizona, USA; page 82: Heather Sugrue ©Blackbirch Press, Inc.; page 84: Courtesy of State of New Hampshire Tourism; page 86: Courtesy of Fallon Convention and Visitors Center; page 88: ©Gregory G. Dimijian 1992/Photo Researchers, Inc.; page 90: Henryk Kaiser/Leo de Wys, Inc.; page 94: James P. Blair/National Geographic Image Collection; page 96: Robyn Horn/Arkansas Department of Parks and Tourism; page 98: ©Rick Golt/Photo Researchers; page 100: ©Barbara Mallette/Leadville Picture Company; page 102: Alaska Division of Tourism; page 104: North Carolina Travel and Tourism; page 108: Alaska Division of Tourism/NPS/David Cohen; page 110: Dick Hamilton Photo ©White Mountain News Bureau/State of New Hampshire Tourism; page 112: ©Jane Dove Juneau; page 116: ©Cecil W. Stoughton/National Park Service; page 118: Permission granted by the Missouri Division of Tourism; page 120: ©William Clark/National Park Service; pages 138, 152: M. Woodbridge Williams/National Park Service; page 140: Phoenix and Valley of the Sun Convention and Visitors Bureau; page 142: National Park Service; page 144: Richard Frear/National Park Service; page 146: ©Jeff Greenberg/dMRp/Photo Researchers, Inc.; page 148: T.C. Gray/National Park Service; page 150: LeRoy Preudhomme/National Park Service; page 154: Robert Holmes/California Division of Tourism; page 156: W.E. Dutton/National Park Service; pages 162, 164: David A. Harvey/© National Geographic Society; pages 166, 178: National Park Service; page 168: ©John W. Bova/Photo Researchers, Inc.; page 176: John Telford/Photo courtesy of the Utah Travel Counci; page 182: ©Carl M. Purcell '95/Photo Researchers, Inc.; page 184: ©George Ranall/Photo Researchers, Inc.; page 186: ©Steve Terrill/Oregon Tourism; page 188: Louisiana Office of Tourism; page 192: ©92 Elder Photo/Call 1-800-BUCKEYE for Ohio Travel Information; page 194: Courtesy of Red River Waterway Commission; page 196: ©Gary Retherford/Photo Researchers, Inc.; page 200: ©Steve Krasema/Photo Researchers, Inc.; page 210: ©Leo de Wys/Leo de Wys, Inc.; page 212: Courtesy of Beers Construction Company; page 214: Superstock Photo, Inc.; page 216: George F. Mobley/National Geographic Image Collection; page 218: ©1992 PeterSkinner/Photo Researchers, Inc.